PASSPORT TO LIFE
Explore God's Word
Experience God's Blessings

France B. Brown, Jr.

Passport to Life
Explore God's Word
Experience God's Blessings

France B. Brown, Jr.

Published and Printed by OXYGEN Press
Houston, TX

978-0-9863841-0-3

To John L. Byrd and R. Elliott Greene

For my passport

Table of Contents

Historical & Cultural Background Tools
Word Study Tools
Biblical Reference Tools
Magnificent 7
Connecting Words
Figures of Speech
Laws of Structure
Literary Forms
Commentary (Colossians 2:16-19)

Life at the Port

Mike and Linda, two of my closest and dearest friends prepared to go on a cruise. The trip's 14 day itinerary included stops in Mexico, Costa Rica, Panama, Columbia and Florida. They flew from Texas to San Diego a full day before the ship was to leave to avoid any last minute problems. On the day of the cruise, they arrived at the port well in advance to board the ship. With smiles of excitement and anticipation they surrendered their luggage and presented their tickets. It didn't take long for their excitement to morph into confusion then bewilderment and ultimately to crushing disappointment. You see, new government regulations required passengers to present passports in order to travel to some of the places on their itinerary. A passport is something that grants access and admission into places we could not go otherwise. Neither Mike nor Linda had a passport. Despite the protest that their travel agent misinformed them, Mike and Linda were not allowed to board the ship and go on the cruise.

For many Christians, Mike and Linda's ordeal is their story. I don't mean their vacation experiences. I'm talking about how they experience life on a daily basis. For far too many believers, life is little more than a series of mishaps, defeats and disappointments.

Passport Required

To be sure, life can be difficult (Rom. 5:3), but it was never meant to be the hopeless grind and empty existence that many believers endure. Jesus said, *I came that they may have life, and have it abundantly* (John 10:10). He came to provide for us a quality salvation experience; one that delivers us from the ports of discontent, disappointment, discouragement and despair. So we've been called to board the ship of life and journey with God. Yes, God wants to take us on a journey; a magnificent journey, from hopelessness to hope, from emptiness to fulfillment, from worry to peace, from failure to victory, from regrets about the past to anticipation about the future, from resentment to acceptance, from darkness to light. Would you like to go? Well, you'll need a passport.

Passport to Life

The *Passport to Life* is a guidebook for exploring God's Word using the Transformational Bible Study methods of observation, interpretation and application. The visas (chapters) include a definition, a discussion and a description of sound and proven methods for interpreting Scripture and applying biblical principles to everyday living. Additionally, each visa (chapter) concludes with an exploration section giving opportunities for personal practice. It is therefore, a spiritual process that gives access and admission into experiencing the blessings of God in awesome and authentic ways.

It is my prayer that as you approach each visa (chapter) that you take a chance on God. Allow Him to work through your anxieties, feelings of inadequacy and moments of doubt. He knows exactly where you are and will work through your brokenness to His glory and to your good. I am convinced beyond the possibility of doubt that should you give yourself to God on this journey, you will never be the same. You will live with stronger faith, greater hope and a deeper love for God, for others and for yourself (Mark 12:30-31).

Bon Voyage!

For Ezra had set his heart to study the law of the LORD and to practice it, and to teach His statutes and ordinances in Israel.

-Ezra 7:10-

All Aboard: Introduction to Transformational Bible Study

`Transformational Bible Study

Definition

Transformational Bible Study is the investigation and application of God's special revelation (2 Tim. 3:16-17; 2 Pet. 1:19-21) based on exegetical (historical, cultural, literary) and theological interpretation (Ezra 7:10; Neh. 8:1-8; Acts 17:11; 1 Pet. 1:23-25) personalized to human needs for the purpose of life transformation (Mark 12:30-31; Rom. 12:2; 1Tim. 1:5).

Discussion

Transformational Bible Study is a holistic process. It follows the pattern of Ezra who the Bible declares studied, embraced and practiced the law of the Lord (Ezra 7:10). It seeks then to engage the head, the heart and the hands of believers.

Transformational Bible Study involves investigation and application of God's special revelation. God has revealed Himself to mankind in two ways: general revelation and special revelation. General revelation refers to God disclosing Himself through creation and the conscience of man (Rom. 1:18-25) while special revelation points to the more personal and direct disclosure of God through the writings of Scripture. As special revelation, Scripture is God's use of human writers to produce a literary work that is divinely authoritative and inerrant (1 Cor. 14:37).

The process of Transformational Bible Study begins with the methodical study and examination of biblical facts. This investigation includes interpreting the sense and the significance of the historical, cultural and literary contexts of a passage (exegetical interpretation) and progresses to the discovery and validation of biblical principles (theological interpretation). It culminates with the believer practicing biblical truth in everyday living (application). The purpose of this process is the transformation of life not merely the stimulation of thoughts or the reformation of behavior. In general, transformation signifies a life submitted to the will of God (James 4:7; Eph. 5:18), by the power of God (Gal. 5:16), to the glory of God (1Cor. 10:31). More concretely, it refers to the sinner turned saint thinking with God's mind (Phil. 2:5-8), feeling with God's heart (Acts 13:22), acting according to God's will (Rom. 6:12-13) for the sake of God's glory (1 Pet. 4:11).

Description

The steps to Transformational Bible Study are:

1. Passage Review
2. Historical Background Study
3. Book Survey
4. Observation
5. Exegetical Outline
6. Cultural Background Study
7. Literary Study
8. Theological Study
9. Application

TRANSFORMATIONAL BIBLE STUDY

ELEMENTS QUESTIONS	OBSERVATION WHAT DO I SEE?	INTERPRETATION WHAT DOES IT MEAN?	APPLICATION WHAT DO I DO?
FUNCTION	Report the facts	Realize the meaning & truth of the facts	Respond to the truth of the facts
FOCUS	FACTS Who · What · When Where · Why · How	CONTEXTS Historical · Cultural · Literary	Biblical Principles Specific Issue Specific Response
FORMS	Structure Atmosphere Literary Form Terms	EXEGETICAL INTERPRETATION Historical Study Cultural Study Literary Study THEOLOGICAL INTERPRETATION Theological Study	Scrutinize Summarize Principle-ize Personalize

For the interpretation of any biblical text to be valid, it must be consistent with the historical-cultural context of that passage.

-J. Scott Duvall-
-J. Daniel Hays-

Itinerary

- Appreciate the importance of history & culture in Bible interpretation

- Become familiar with tools and resources for performing background studies

- Develop background studies

VISA 1: Historical & Cultural Background Studies

Historical Background

Definition

A Historical Background Study refers to the exploration of information related to the author and audience of a Bible book.

Discussion

The books of the Bible portray real people in real historical situations. In order to discover the author's intent to and for the original audience, the Bible student must investigate and understand the historical context in which a book was written. To this end, consult the research tools listed in the appendix to answer the questions below.

The Author

- Lineage: Who were the author's relatives and ancestors? How did the author benefit from or suffer for being a member of a particular culture?

- Location: Where was the author located? What was the place like?

- Learning: By whom, where, how, in what and to what extent was the author educated?

- Livelihood: What was the author's vocation or means for financial support?

- Landmark Moments: What are some significant spiritual/religious experiences the author encountered?

The Audience

- People: Who were they? What were they like?

- Place: Where was the audience located? What was the place like?

- Perspective: When was the book written? What was happening during this period in history?

- Problems: What were their particular issues, challenges and situations?

- Purpose: Why was the book written?

Description

The Book of James[1]

The Author:

James, the half-brother of Jesus Christ, is the author according to the majority of scholars, though there are 4 other "James" possibilities.

Astute Greek, Aramaic and Hebrew language skills and accomplished speaker (Acts 15). James knew the Old Testament and he knew Jesus' teachings as evidenced by his use of them throughout his epistle.

Managed (presided over) the Jerusalem Council (Acts 15) to whom Paul, Barnabas and Peter presented their arguments in favor of accepting the Gentiles. A pillar of the church (Gal. 2:9).

Enriched by his Jewish heritage and encouraged by his godly parents (Mary and Joseph), James knew scripture and Hebrew symbolism as evidenced in this epistle.

Suspicious of Jesus' early ministry and unbelieving in him as Christ, James became a "Servant of God and of the Lord Jesus Christ" (James 1:1) after Jesus resurrection and appearance to him (John 7:5 and 1 Cor. 15:7).

The Audience:

Jewish Christians, primarily, and all believers.

Everywhere throughout the Roman Empire. These believers, dispersed from Israel, risked losing everything in order to be faithful to Jesus. Persecution by both the Roman government and the Jews was the order of the day.

When? Probably 45 – 50 A.D. before the Jerusalem Council meeting in Acts 15. Most likely the earliest New Testament writing.

Scattered, tattered and, yet, faithful, these believers needed practical wisdom and teaching in Christian living in a hostile environment, encouragement to endure trials, and hope for Christ's coming again.

Purpose: "But prove yourselves doers of the word, and not merely hearers, who delude themselves." James 1:22

---

[1] Special thanks to Carol Harris for this creative and insightful study.

The Book of Isaiah

The Author:

Lineage: Isaiah (the Lord saves) was the son of Amoz. He was the husband of a prophetess (8:3) and fathered two sons (7:3; 8:3).

Location: Isaiah lived in or near Jerusalem. He ministered and wrote to Judah during a time of political turbulence and spiritual decay.

Learning: Isaiah's impressive vocabulary suggests that he was cultured and well educated. He used various literary devices and poetic expressions to convey his thoughts in striking and appealing ways.

Livelihood: Isaiah was a skillful statesman who demonstrated astute abilities in political affairs. He advised Hezekiah concerning policies toward Assyria (Isa. 37) and Babylon (Isa. 39).

Landmark
Moments: Isaiah was a writing prophet who was commissioned by God in the year of King Uzziah's death (739 B.C.). He urged King Ahaz to trust God in the face of the Aram-Israel alliance that threatened Judah (Isa. 7) and encouraged King Hezekiah when Judah was threatened by Assyria. Jewish tradition claims that Isaiah was sawn in two during the reign of Manasseh the son Hezekiah (cf. Heb. 11:37).

The Audience

People: Two groups were the recipients of Isaiah's message: (1) the generation that strayed from God and drew His discipline of Babylonia captivity and (2) the future generation who would live in captivity as a result of the sins of their fathers.

Place: The recipients of Isaiah's message lived in Judah (the Southern Kingdom). Jerusalem was its capital city.

Perspective: Isaiah ministered during the last years of Israel (the Northern Kingdom) which fell to Assyria in 722 B.C. (2 Kings 18:11-12). He ministered for 58 years during the reigns of four kings: Uzziah (790-739 B.C), Jotham (750-732 B.C), Ahaz (735-715 B.C) and Hezekiah (715-686 B.C).

Problems: Judah was filled with materialism, oppression, religious formality and corruption. She avoided Assyrian domination but her rampant disobedience and irreverence towards God would lead to the punishment of Babylonia captivity.

Purpose: The purpose of Isaiah was to highlight God's glory as the one who judges sin yet comforts His people in the midst of their discipline with His faithfulness to restore them to the land of promise.

Cultural Background

Definition

A Cultural Background Study is an exploration of the social context of biblical material.

Discussion

Culture refers the beliefs, behaviors, customs, norms, arts and institutions that characterize and inform a society. In seeking to discover an author's message to his audience, the Bible student must investigate and understand the cultural factors at play in the author's writing. To this end, consult the reference tools listed in the appendix to find information related to culture. Elements of culture include but are not limited to the following:

- Political: What was the system of government?

- Geographical: Is there significance to the places and particular locals?

- Economic: How was trade conducted?

- Legal: What was the nature and procedures of the judicial system?

- Architectural: What type of buildings were constructed? How? Why?

- Clothing: How did people dress? Why?

- Social: How did people relate to each other? Why?

- Religious/Theological: How did people worship and relate to God? How did God relate to them?

Description

Widows and Orphans (James 1:27)

Widows and orphans were the most vulnerable people in this society. They had no direct means of support or any legal or social advocates. James admonished his Jewish audience that more than Judaism, Christianity was expressed through acts of benevolent affection to the most vulnerable and needy in society.

Sackcloth and Barefoot (Isaiah 20:2)

The sackcloth was a dark outer garment made from goat's hair and was worn by mourners. Prophets also wore sackcloth to symbolize their preached message of repentance. Going barefoot was a sign of poverty and reproach. For three years Isaiah walked in this condition as an object lesson of how Egypt and Cush would be treated by Assyria.

Exploration

Research the Historical Background of the following Bible books.

1. Malachi

2. Luke

3. 1 Thessalonians

4. 1 Peter

5. Revelation

Research the following elements of Cultural Background.

1. Describe the responsibilities of the priests in Malachi and discuss the significance of their attitudes and actions in Malachi 1:6-8?

2. Discuss the Feast of Unleavened Bread/Passover in Luke 22:1.

3. How does Paul use the concept of crown in 1 Thessalonians 2:19?

4. Explain the image of shepherd in 1 Peter 5:2 and discuss its significance.

5. Discuss the spiritual climate of the city of Sardis in Revelation 3:1.

One of the greatest ways to summarize material is to put it in the form of a chart, especially when you need to visualize a lot of material.

-Howard G. Hendricks-

Itinerary

- Appreciate the value of charting biblical material

- Learn the process of charting

- Practice charting a Bible book

VISA 2: Book Charting (Survey)

Book Charting (Survey)

Definition

A Book Chart is a visual representation of the synthesized information of a Bible book.

Discussion

A chart is useful for organizing, summarizing, analyzing and visualizing large segments of biblical material. In other words it allows you to see how the parts contribute to and fit with the whole. There are three major elements to a book chart: divisions, sections and themes.

- Divisions are the largest units of material in which a book may be broken down. Usually, a book is broken down into three divisions.

- Sections are the smaller segments of material that make up the divisions. Put another way, a division can be broken down into two or more sections. Sections are developed from the individual paragraphs of a book.

- Themes are the dominant, recurring or unifying subjects, thoughts or ideas discussed in a division of material.

Process

1. Summarize each paragraph in the book (1-3 sentences). For larger books, you may summarize the chapters.

2. Title each paragraph (2-5 words).

3. Group titled paragraphs into three divisions.

   - Combine paragraphs that are similar in thought.

   - Tip: Look at Laws of Structure between paragraphs (see appendix).

   - Tip: Look at Connecting Words between paragraphs (see appendix).

   - Tip: Look at "breaks" between paragraphs.

4. Title each of the three divisions and indicate their Scripture references.

5. Within each division, group the paragraphs into Sections (2-5). Find the dominant theme in each division.

6. Summarize the entire book in one sentence (20 words or less) and give the chart a title.

7. Draw a blank chart. If you use a computer program, you may draw your chart using an 8 ½ x 11 sheet of paper (landscape orientation). If you draw it by hand, you will want to use a larger page.

8. Record the information that you have gathered in the appropriate areas of the chart (see below). Please note, you will not record the descriptions only titles and Scripture references. Scripture references for sections should be written in the same slot as section titles. Place the verse number that begins the section to the left of the title and the verse number that ends the section to the right of the title.

Description

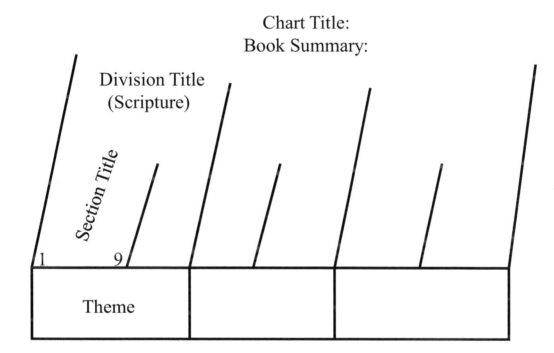

Chart Title:
Book Summary:

Jonah: Issues of the Heart

God's sovereignty and grace demands a faithful response.

Tough Heart (1:1-16)	Thankful Heart (1:17-2:10)	Tainted Heart (3-4)
Jonah: "I'm Bad"	A Fish Story	2nd Time Around
Jonah... Busted!	On Dry Ground	School Daze
"Who's Da Man"		
God & Disobedience (1:1-4, 10-13)	Trouble (2:1-7)	God & Faithfulness (3)
God & Obedience (1:14-16)	Thanksgiving (2:8-9)	God & Unfaithfulness (4)

Verse markers: 1, 3, 4, 9, 10, 16, 1:17, 2:9, 2:10, 3:1, 10, 4:1, 11

Tsunami from Heaven

Acts traces the establishment and rapid progression of God's church.

Church Established (1-7)			Church Extended (8-12)			Church Expanded (13-28)	
By the Holy Spirit	Through Peter	In Persecution	Through Persecution	Through Saul's Conversion	Through Peter's Ministry	Through Paul's Service	Through Paul's Suffering
1:1	14 15	4:22 23	7:60 8:1	40 9:1	31 32	12:25 3:1	21:16 17 28:31
Local Jerusalem			Regional Judea & Samaria			Viral Remotest Parts	

19

Exploration

Develop charts of the following books of the Bible.

1. Ruth

2. Joel

3. Ephesians

4. Mark

5. Romans

Itinerary

- Learn principles & practices of identifying biblical facts

- Understanding the importance of paragraphs

- Practice identifying and reporting biblical facts

VISA 3: Observation

21

Observation

Definition

An Observation is a statement that reports the facts of the biblical text.

Discussion

To observe is to read and make note of the facts (who, what, when, where, why and how) of the text. These facts are indicated in the following elements of a passage:

- **Structure** refers to how the author arranged his thoughts and words.

- **Atmosphere** refers to the dominant mood or tone of the passage (joy, thanksgiving, despair, urgency, etc.).

- **Literary Form** refers to the category to which the passage belongs. Put another way, it is the type or kind (genre) of writing that the passage characterizes.

- **Terms** refers to words used in Scripture.

Observations answer the question "What do I see?" or "What does the text say?" The following guidelines will help in *seeing* and reporting good observations.

- Be Prayerful
- Be Purposeful
- Be Patient
- Be Persistent
- Be Plain

A good observation statement reflects the following qualities:

- Reports but does not interpret the facts of the text.

- Reflects the time of the text and avoids reporting that expresses present or future time.

- Reports in a complete declarative sentence avoiding phrases, questions and incomplete thoughts.

- Indicates verse(s) from which the observation is reported.

Description

Read the Bible verses below and review the related observation statements.

Romans 4:17

(as it is written, "A FATHER OF MANY NATIONS HAVE I MADE YOU") in the presence of Him whom he believed, *even* God, who gives life to the dead and calls into being that which does not exist. (NASB)

Observations

1. The audience of the verse is not identified (v. 17).

2. The quoted statement is in parentheses (v. 17).

3. A statement was written (v. 17).

4. The written statement is quoted   (v. 17).

5. The audience of the quoted statement is not identified (v. 17).

6. This thought is related to a previous thought (v. 17).

7. Someone was a father (v.17).

8. Someone made someone else a father (v. 17).

9. The audience of the quote is father of many nations (v. 17).

10. God gives life to the dead (v. 17).

11. The dead exists (v. 17).

12. God calls into being that which does not exist (v.17).

13. Some things don't exist (v. 17).

14. Someone believed in Him (v. 17).

15. "Him" has presence (v. 17).

Daniel 1:8-13

[8] But Daniel made up his mind that he would not defile himself with the king's choice food or with the wine which he drank; so he sought *permission* from the commander of the officials that he might not defile himself. [9] Now God granted Daniel favor and compassion in the sight of the commander of the officials, [10] and the commander of the officials said to Daniel, "I am afraid of my lord the king, who has appointed your food and your drink; for why should he see your faces looking more haggard than the youths who are your own age? Then you would make me forfeit my head to the king." [11] But Daniel said to the overseer whom the commander of the officials had appointed over Daniel, Hananiah, Mishael and Azariah, [12] "Please test your servants for ten days, and let us be given some vegetables to eat and water to drink. [13] "Then let our appearance be observed in your presence and the appearance of the youths who are eating the king's choice food; and deal with your servants according to what you see." (NASB)

Observations

1.   An account/story is told (vv. 8-13).

2.   Daniel determined not to defile himself with food and drink (v. 8).

3.   Daniel sought permission from the commander not to defile himself (v. 8).

4.   The commander was over the officials (v. 8).

5.   God gave Daniel favor and compassion with the commander (v. 9).

6.   The king appointed food and drink for Daniel, Hananiah, Mishael and Azariah (vv. 10-11).

7.   The commander expressed his fear of death to Daniel (v. 10).

8.   Daniel, Hananiah, Mishael and Azariah are youths (v. 10).

9.   The commander had authority over what Daniel, Hananiah, Mishael and Azariah ate (vv. 8-10).

10.   The commander did not give permission to Daniel not to defile himself (v. 10).

11.   The commander appointed an overseer to Daniel, Hananiah, Mishael and Azariah (v. 11).

12.   Daniel sought permission from the overseer despite not receiving permission from the commander defile himself (v. 11).

13.   Daniel requested that Hananiah, Mishael, Azariah and he be given vegetables and water (v. 12).

14.   Daniel requested that the overseer test them for ten days concerning their diet (vv. 11-12).

15.   Daniel referred to the other three youths and himself as servants (v. 13).

Paragraphs

Definition

A paragraph is a portion of a larger body of written material that consists of one or more sentences and expresses one main thought.

Discussion

The paragraph plays a central role in the study of Scripture because it is the immediate literary context of a passage. As such, the paragraph is seen as the *basic unit of study* (BUS). In other words, the paragraph is the starting point for study. Important facts to remember about the paragraph include the following:

- It is part of a larger composition
- It is made up of one or more sentences
- It expresses a central idea or single dominant thought (big idea)

Paragraphs are identified in Scripture in several different ways.

- Paragraph markers (NASB, KJV, NKJ)
- Verse numbers in bold (NASB,NIV)
- Clustered type-setting (NIV, NKJ)

Description

The following are examples of paragraph markers and paragraphs found in some English Bibles.

2 Corinthians 7:1 (KJV)

¶[1]Therefore, having these promises, beloved, let us cleanse ourselves from all defilement of flesh and spirit, perfecting holiness in the fear of God.

James 5:19-20 (NASB)

[19] My brethren, if any among you strays from the truth, and one turns him back,
[20] let him know that he who turns a sinner from the error of his way will save his soul from death, and will cover a multitude of sins.

2 Samuel 4:1-4 (NIV)

[1]When Ish-Bosheth son of Saul heard that Abner had died in Hebron, he lost courage, and all Israel became alarmed. [2] Now Saul's son had two men who were leaders of raiding bands. One was named Baanah and the other Recab; they were sons of Rimmon the Beerothite from the tribe of Benjamin–Beeroth is considered part of Benjamin, [3] because the people of Beeroth fled to Gittaim and have lived there as aliens to this day.

[4] (Jonathan son of Saul had a son who was lame in both feet. He was five years old when the news about Saul and Jonathan came from Jezreel. His nurse picked him up and fled, but as she hurried to leave, he fell and became crippled. His name was Mephibosheth.).

Exploration

Read and develop 15-50 observations from each of the following passages.

1. John 3:16

2. Matthew 28:18-20

3. Ecclesiastes 5:1-7

4. 2 John 1-13

5. 2 Samuel 6:1-11

Probably the most helpful form of structural analysis is to produce a sentence-flow schematic. This is a simplified form of diagramming whose purpose is to depict graphically by coordination and by indention and subordination the relation between words and clauses in a passage.

-Gordon D. Fee-

Itinerary

- Learn the principles & practices of developing mechanical layouts

- Learn the process of analyzing the grammatical flow of a passage

- Practice developing mechanical layouts

VISA 4: Mechanical Layout

Mechanical Layout

Definition

A Mechanical Layout is a graphic representation of the grammatical flow of the author's thinking as reflected in a portion of Scripture.

Discussion

Purpose

A Mechanical Layout graphically illustrates how an author grammatically arranged the words of a passage. While it can be useful in other genres, it is especially suited for study in the Epistles. It helps the Bible student:

- trace the flow of the author's thinking
- clearly see grammatical associations
- note order of discussion
- observe the emphasis of the text
- identify key clauses, phrases and words
- ask and answer exegetical questions (see VISA 6)

Process

The process of developing a Mechanical Layout is based on positioning by subordination and indentation. This allows the student to see how thoughts are connected. Complete thoughts are identified and recorded from the left margin of a page. Then incomplete thoughts are identified, written underneath the complete thought and indented.
The following sentence is made up of two thoughts (clauses): one complete (independent clause) and one incomplete (dependent clause).

I love studying the Bible because it gives me power and insights for living.

A layout for this sentence would look like this:

I love studying the Bible (complete)
       because it gives me power and insights for living. (incomplete)

In this case, the incomplete thought gives the reason for the complete thought. Incomplete thoughts modify complete thoughts as well as other incomplete thoughts by describing, limiting or in some way characterizing them.

This subordination and indentation process is based on identifying these markers:

- main verbs and their complete thoughts (independent clauses)
- verbs and their incomplete thoughts (dependent clauses)
- Connecting Words

Preparation

1.   Use 8 ½ x 11 (or larger) plain white paper (landscape orientation).

2.   Use pencil as you will likely make several changes. You can type it later.

3.   Instead, you may develop the layout directly from your computer by cutting and pasting the passage from a Bible software program or simply by typing the words of the passage.

Process

4.   Identify the first complete thought in your passage.

- Look for the main/controlling verb.
- Look for the Connecting Words: for, and, therefore, now, etc.
- Record the complete thought at the left margin of the page.

5.   Identify the incomplete thoughts that relate to the complete thought.

- Look for Connecting Words: that, so that, for, as, etc.
- Look for participles.
- Look for verbs within the incomplete thought.
- Place this thought under the complete thought (subordination).
- Indent the incomplete thought.
- More than one incomplete thought may relate to the same complete thought.

6.   Identify incomplete thoughts that relate to the above incomplete thought by following the same process of subordination and indention.

7.   Repeat Steps 4-6 until the passage is completed.

Description

John 3:16

[16]"For God so loved the world,
    that He gave His only begotten Son,
        that whoever believes in Him should not perish,
            but have eternal life.

Matthew 28:18-20

[18]And Jesus came up and spoke to them, saying,
  "All authority has been given to Me in heaven and on earth.
[19]"Go therefore
  and make disciples of all the nations,
    baptizing them in the name of the Father
      and the Son
      and the Holy Spirit,
[20]teaching them to observe all that I commanded you;
and lo,
I am with you always,
  even to the end of the age."

Romans 12:1-2

[1]Therefore
I urge you, brethren,
  by the mercies of God,
    to present your bodies a living
        and
      holy sacrifice,
        acceptable to God,
          which is your spiritual service of worship.

[2]And
do not be conformed to this world,
but
be transformed
    by the renewing of your mind,
      that you may prove what the will of God is,
          that which is good
              and
            acceptable
              and
                perfect.

1 Thessalonians 2:5-12

5For we never came with flattering speech
  as you know,
  nor with a pretext for greed
      --God is witness--
6nor did we seek glory from men
  either from you or from others
      even though as apostles of Christ we might have asserted our authority.
7But we proved to be gentle among you,
      as a nursing mother tenderly cares for her own children.

8 having thus a fond affection for you,
we were well-pleased to impart to you not only the gospel of God but also our own lives
      because you had become very dear to us.
9For you recall, brethren, our labor and hardship,
      how working night and day
            so as not to be a burden to any of you,
      we proclaimed to you the gospel of God.
10You are witnesses,
  and so is God,
      how devoutly
      and uprightly
      and blamelessly
            we behaved toward you believers;
11just as you know how we were exhorting
  and encouraging
  and imploring each one of you
      as a father would his own children.
            12so that you may walk in a manner worthy of the God
                  who calls you into His own kingdom and glory.

32

Exploration

Develop Mechanical Layouts from the following passages.

1. Romans 1:16-17

2. Hebrews 4:14-16

3. Matthew 5:3-11

4. James 1:21-27

5. Ephesians 5:22-32

Itinerary

- Learn the principles & practices of outlining a passage

- Appreciate the value of outlining

- Practice outlining

VISA 5: Exegetical Outline

Exegetical Outline

Definition

The Exegetical Outline is a one page document that reflects how the original author arranged biblical material. The arrangement of biblical material is known as structure.

Discussion

Preparation: Read the passage

1. Read the passage at least 3 times.

2. Write at least 20-30 Observations.

Process: Outline the passage

3. Print a copy of your passage so that you may write on it.

4. Identify major changes in thoughts, topics, discussions, scenes and/or characters. Pay attention to Connecting Words. Draw a circle around the verse numbers where major changes begin.

5. Label major changes with Roman numerals (I., II., III., IV., V., etc.). These major changes are the Major Points that will serve as the skeleton of your outline.

6. Within each Major Point from above, there are changes in thoughts, topics, discussions, scenes and/or characters. Identify these minor changes by underlining or highlighting the first word in the verse where the minor change begins. Pay attention to Connecting Words. Label them with capital letters (A., B., C., D., E., etc.). These are now the Minor Points of your outline.

7. On a separate page, summarize each Major Point in a complete sentence. Your summaries must be identified by the appropriate Roman numeral, reference the author and the audience of the book, be written in the past tense and include proper verse references (see examples at the end of this lesson).

8. In a complete sentence, summarize each Minor Point within its corresponding Major Point. Your summaries must be identified by the appropriate letter of the alphabet, reference the author and the audience of the book, be written in the past tense and include proper verse reference (see examples at the end of this lesson).

9. Summarize the entire passage in one complete sentence using 20 words or less. This summary is the Exegetical Big Idea (the original author's message to the original audience). The statement must reference the author and the audience of the book and be written in the past tense (see examples at the end of this lesson). Your summary as well as your outline will likely undergo some revision after you have performed more in-depth study on the passage.

Presentation: Write the outline

10. On a separate page, type the summary of Major Point I. On the line below this summary, indent and type the summary of Minor Point A. Directly below Minor Point A., type the summary of Minor Point B. Repeat this process with all remaining Minor Points of Major Point I.

11. Repeat the above step until you have completed the entire passage.

12. Type passage summary (Exegetical Big Idea) at the top of the page.

13. Give the outline a title and place it at the top of the page.

14. Note: Do not rearrange or omit verses.

15. Note that having a Major Point I. requires that you have a Major Point II.

16. Note that having a Minor Point A. requires that you have a Minor Point B.

17. Note that sometimes it may be necessary to breakdown Minor Points into Sub-Points. Sub-Points are more detailed summaries of Minor Points. They are indicated by Arabic numbers (1., 2., 3., etc.). A Sub-point 1 requires a Sub-Point 2.

Description

Soldiers of Love
Philippians 2:19-30

Exegetical Big Idea: Paul expressed his, Timothy's and Epaphroditus' love to the Philippians and admonished them to honor those committed to Christ.

I. Paul expressed his affection to the Philippians by desiring to send Timothy and to see them himself (vv. 19-24).

    A. Paul told the Philippians of his hope to learn of their condition through sending Timothy to them (v. 19).

    B. Paul told the Philippians the reason he wanted to send Timothy was because he would be genuinely concerned about them (v. 20).

    C. Paul told the Philippians that others sought after their own interests (v. 21).

    D. Paul reminded the Philippians that Timothy served with him in the furtherance of the gospel (v. 22).

    E. Paul reemphasized to the Philippians his desire to send Timothy (v. 23).

    F. Paul expressed to the Philippians his desire to see them (v. 24).

II. Paul told the Philippians that he was sending Epaphroditus as an encouragement to Epaphroditus and them (vv. 25-28).

    A. Paul told the Philippians that he was sending Epaphroditus (v. 25).

        1. Paul described Epaphroditus to the Philippians as his brother (v. 25a).

        2. Paul described Epaphroditus to the Philippians as his fellow worker (v. 25b).

        3. Paul described Epaphroditus to the Philippians as his fellow soldier (v. 25c).

        4. Paul described Epaphroditus to the Philippians as their minister to his need (v. 25d).

        5. Paul described Epaphroditus to the Philippians as their messenger to his need (v. 25e).

    B. Paul told the Philippians the reason he was sending Epaphroditus was because he was concerned for them (vv. 26-27).

        1. Paul told the Philippians that Epaphroditus longed for them (v. 26).

        2. Paul explained to the Philippians the extent of Epaphroditus' sickness (v. 27).

    C. Paul told the Philippians his own reasons for sending Epaphroditus was so that they would rejoice and he would be less concerned for them (v. 28).

III. Paul told the Philippians to honor Epaphroditus and men like him because of their commitment (vv. 29-30).

    A. Paul told the Philippians to receive Epaphroditus with joy (v. 29a).

    B. Paul told the Philippians to honor men like Epaphroditus (v. 29b).

    C. Paul told the Philippians the reason they should honor Epaphroditus was because he almost died serving in ministry (v. 30).

Broken for the Better
Genesis 32:22-32

Exegetical Big Idea: Moses told the Israelites that God opposed Jacob because of his self-will and then blessed him because of his humility.

I.   Moses told the Israelites that Jacob crossed the ford Jabbok and sent all of his resources and family across the stream (vv. 22-23).

II.   Moses told the Israelites that a man fought against Jacob (vv. 24-25).

    A.   Moses told the Israelites that while Jacob was alone a man wrestled with him until daybreak (v. 24).

    B.   Moses told the Israelites that the man dislocated Jacob's thigh while they wrestled (v. 25).

III.   Moses told the Israelites that Jacob was blessed by the man (vv. 26-29).

    A.   Moses told the Israelites that Jacob requested a blessing from the man after he would not let him go (v. 26).

    B.   Moses told the Israelites that Jacob confessed his name to the man upon his request (v. 27).

    C.   Moses told the Israelites that Jacob was given a new name by the man (v. 28).

    D.   Moses told the Israelites that Jacob was denied the request of knowing the name of the man who blessed him (v. 29).

IV.   Moses told the Israelites that Jacob responded to his blessing from the man by naming the place Peniel ("the face of God") (v. 30).

V.   Moses told the Israelites that the sun rose on Jacob as he crossed over Penuel limping (v. 31).

VI.   Moses told the Israelites the reason the sons of Israel don't eat the socket of the thigh was because Jacob's thigh was injured (v. 32).

Exploration

Develop Exegetical Outlines of the following passages.

1. Hebrews 4:14-16

2. Revelation 2:1-7

3. Numbers 12:1-16

4. Nehemiah 4:1-23

5. Ephesians 5:22-32

...there is no one-size-fits-all approach to interpreting Scripture.

-David M. Howard, Jr.-

Itinerary

- Learn the meaning of interpretation (Exegetical & Theological)

- Become familiar with the significance of the various types of contexts of Scripture

- Learn the processes of interpretation (Exegetical & Theological)

VISA 6: Principles of Interpretation

Exegetical Interpretation

Definition

Exegetical Interpretation is discovering the meaning of a biblical passage according to the original author's intent for the original audience.

Discussion

The goal of Exegetical Interpretation is to discover the message of the original author. The guidelines that follow are proven strategies for doing this in an accurate and thorough way.

1. Interpret by asking and answering exegetical questions. This is the means to interpretation. Exegetical questions are investigative inquiries designed to probe the facts of the text for meaning. Use the following interrogatives to develop and apply exegetical questions to the various contexts of a passage:

   - Who
   - What
   - When

   - Where
   - Why
   - How

   - Examples from Matthew 28:18-20:

     - Why did Matthew include this passage in the book?

     - Who was Jesus talking to? (v. 18)

     - What is the meaning of "authority?" (v. 18)

     - Where is Jesus and His audience? (v. 18)

     - When did the events of the passage take place?

     - What is a disciple? Why did Jesus use this term? What are the implications for Jesus, His listeners and the nations? (v. 19)

     - How are they to make disciples? (vv. 19-20)

     - What is the significance of "baptizing?" (v. 19)

     - What is the relationship between verse 18 and 19… between verse 19 and 20?

     - What did Jesus promise His listeners? (v. 20)

2. Interpret in light of the various contexts of a passage.

- Context refers to the interrelated elements of a passage that give it meaning and allows it to be accurately understood.

- Historical Context refers to the circumstances and conditions of the passage related to its original author and audience (see VISA 1).

- Cultural Context refers to the circumstances and conditions of the passage related to a society's way of life. (see VISA 1).

- Literary Context refers to the biblical material that precede, follow and give meaning to the words, phrases, clauses and sentences of a passage. It is made of **SALT**.

  - **S**tructure refers to the logical arrangement of biblical material (see Laws of Structure in the appendix).

  - **A**tmosphere refers to the dominant mood or tone of a passage (joy, thanksgiving, despair, urgency, etc.).

  - **L**iterary Form refers to the genre of a passage (narrative, poetry, epistle, prophetic, apocalyptic, etc.). See Literary Forms in the appendix.

  - **T**erms are words and word groups used in Scripture.

3. Interpret according to the correct use of words and word groups.

- A word communicates nothing by itself. It needs to be used in connection with other words in order for it to have meaning ("lion" Rev. 5:5 and 1 Pet. 5:8).

- Words change meaning over time---1 Thess. 4:15 "prevent" (KJV) vs. "precede" (NASB).

- A particular word maybe used differently in other parts of Scripture or by the same author. In John 3:17, "world" is used three times in two different ways.

- Some word uses are unique to the Bible. In Scripture "death" refers to separation not cessation.

- Physical (Josh. 24:29)

- Spiritual (Gen. 2:15-17; 3:23-24)

- Eternal (Rev. 20:13-15)

- Focus on the keywords (see Magnificent 7 in the appendix).

- Ask: "What does this word or word group mean in context?" or "How does the author or speaker use this word or word group?"

4. Interpret according to the original author's intent for the original audience.

- Consider the occasion of the writing.

- Consider the author's purpose for writing.

- Ask: "Why does the author or speaker use this word or word group this way to these people at this time?"

- Ask: "What are the implications of the reason the author or speaker used this word or word group?" In other words, what does the author or speaker's rationale for using a word or word group communicate about the author and audience or the speaker and listeners and the conditions and circumstances of the text.

- Implications are natural conclusions and legitimate inferences drawn from sound investigation of the text although something may not be explicitly stated.

Description

Synthesize discoveries using three documents: (1) a verse-by-verse paraphrase of the passage, (2) revised Exegetical Outline and (3) a passage commentary (1-2 pages).

Exegetical Synthesis

- Paraphrase (cover page)

- Exegetical Outline (revised)

- Passage Commentary (see appendix)

  - Explanation

  - Exploration

Theological Interpretation

Definition

Theological Interpretation is discovering the Holy Spirit's timeless and universal message of a biblical passage.

Discussion

The Holy Scriptures are ancient writings that began over 3000 years ago (Old Testament 1400 BC-400 BC and New Testament AD 40-AD 96). They were influenced by, reflective of and directed towards the history, culture and language of their day. Although we interpret the early contexts, we cannot apply them to our lives today because the particular circumstances and conditions of the text are different from our own. How then do we engage the ancient text so that it is not merely descriptive of the past but prescriptive for our present and future?

Theological Interpretation is the cable that connects the Word of God to the people of God. Its purpose is to discover the message of the Holy Spirit to all people, in all places, in all circumstances for all time periods. To be sure, the Bible declares that the Word of God originated from the Spirit of God. It was the Holy Spirit who moved men to speak from God (2 Pet. 1:21) and superintended the writings of the human authors (2 Tim. 3:16). In the Old Testament, the prophets spoke by means of the Holy Spirit (2 Sam. 23:3; Ezek. 2:2; Micah 3:8). In the New Testament, Scripture is recognized as the work of the Holy Spirit (Acts 28:25; Heb. 3:7; 10:15-17). His message is expressed in theological principles which are statements of abiding and enduring truth. They may also be referred to as: timeless truths, biblical truths, biblical principles or life lessons. This signifies that the Bible is forever active and authoritative.

Description

Jesus and the apostles practiced theological interpretation when they interpreted the literal meaning of the Old Testament, understood its timeless and universal relevance and related it in principle statements to new situations. In Mark 12:30-31, Jesus took the 613 specific commands of the Old Testament that were condensed in the Ten Commandments and summarized them in two commandments. In responding to the temptations of Satan in Matthew 4:1-11, Jesus applied principles from Scripture whose original audience was Israel (Deut. 8:3; 6:16-17; 6:13). In 1 Peter 1:23-25, the apostle characterized the Word of God as perpetually productive and powerful. He supported his assertion by appealing to Isaiah 40:6-8. In these examples, Jesus and Peter discovered the theological principles of the ancient writings and applied them to their specific situations.

Discoveries from Theological Interpretation will be reflected in the Theological Outline.

Theological Outline

Definition

The Theological Outline is a one page document that reflects the Holy Spirit's timeless and universal principles of the passage.

Discussion

Preparation

1. Review your passage commentary.

Process

2. Print a copy of your Exegetical Outline so that you may use it as a worksheet.

3. Discover the Theological Big Idea of the passage.

   - Apply the following theological questions to the Exegetical Big Idea:

   - "What does the Exegetical Big Idea teach about God?"
     (How does He think, feel and/or act?)

   - "What does the Exegetical Big Idea teach about mankind?"
     (How do people tend to think, feel and/or act?)

   - "What does the Exegetical Big Idea teach about life in general?"
     (How does life tend to work?)

   - When considering these questions, you must remember that God is Holy (1 Pet. 1:16), man is depraved (Rom 3:23) and life is imperfect (Rom. 8:18).

4. Principle-ize your answers.

   - Record your answers as principle statements using universal and timeless language.

   - Drop all historical and cultural references.

   - Begin your statements with *"All Christians Should..."*

   - Example:

     - Exegetical: "**Moses told the Israelites** that God would bless their obedience."

     - Theological: "**All Christians should know** that God blesses obedience."

5. Validate your statements.

- Cross reference at least three other passages from the rest of Scripture that legitimately support your assertions by way of expression, explanation, exhortation and/or example.

- Include one passage from the Bible book you are studying.

- Use the following tools to help locate relevant passages: study Bible, topical Bible, concordance or commentary.

6. Select the statement that is most appropriate to your passage.

7. Discover the theological principle for Main Point I of the Exegetical Outline.

- Repeat Steps 1-6.

8. Discover the theological principles for each of the Minor Points corresponding to Main Point I.

- Repeat Steps 1-6 for each Minor Point related to Major Point I.

- Every Minor Point does not communicate a theological principle on its own. It may need to be combined and summarized with those directly before or after it.

9. Repeat Steps 1-8 for each of the remaining Major and Minor Points of the Exegetical Outline.

Presentation

10. At the top of a separate page, type the Scripture reference and Theological Big Idea. Include the validation Scriptures in parenthesis.

11. For the body of your outline, type Major and Minor Points with the validation Scriptures for each in parentheses. Do not rearrange or omit verses. Remember that Major Point I. requires that you have a Major Point II and Minor Point A. requires that you have Minor Point B.

Description

Review the following Theological Outline of Genesis 32:22-32 with the Exegetical Outline of the same passage in VISA 5.

Theological Outline

Genesis 32:22-32

Theological Big Idea: All Christians should know that God opposes the self-will of man but favors humility. (Gen. 3:11-24; Psalm 138:6; James 4:6)

I.   All Christians should know that self-reliance is destructive (vv. 22-23). (Gen. 32:1-21; Matt. 6:24-34; 19:16-23)

II.   All Christians should know that God opposes man's self-dependence (vv. 24-25). (Gen. 3:11-24; Matt. 19:16-23; James 4:6)

III.   All Christians should know that God responds favorably to humility (vv. 26-29). (Gen. 22:9-19; Phil. 4:6-7; James 4:6)

IV.   All Christians should express gratitude for God's grace (v. 30). (Gen. 22:14; Psalm 117; Phil. 4:6)

V.   All Christians should yield to the authority of God (v.v. 31-32). (Gen. 6:22; Prov. 3:5-6; James 4:6)

Itinerary

- Value the power of biblical poetry for Christian living

- Learn the principles and processes for interpreting biblical poetry

- Practice interpreting biblical poetry

VISA 7: Interpreting Biblical Poetry

Proverbs

Definition

Proverbs are short memorable statements of truth based on real life experience. They are simple yet profound seeking to make permanent the truths about living life wisely/righteously.

Discussion

The Hebrew Bible titles this book The Proverbs of Solomon, the Son of David, King in Israel (cf. 1:1; 1 Kings 4:32). The Septuagint (the Greek translation of the Old Testament) used the title The Proverbs of Solomon. Our English use of the title comes from the Latin Vulgate title of The Book of Proverbs.

Proverbs showed the Israelites how they should respond to God in their everyday living. Its purpose was to help God's people live wisely and skillfully. Thus the nature of Proverbs relates to principles to live by not necessarily promises to claim. Biblically speaking, being wise starts with a proper view of God and right relationship with God (1:7).

Description

Although it is a collection of wise sayings, the book of Proverbs reflects structural and thematic unity. It can be divided into at least six sections.

I.   Words to the Wise (1-9)[2]

II.   Solomon's Sayings (10:17-22:16)

III.   Sages Speak (22:17-24:34)

IV.   Hezekiah's Help with Solomon's Sayings (25-29)

V.   Agur's Admonitions (30)

VI.   Last Words by Lemuel (31)

---

[2] Scholars differ on the writers of chapters 1-9. Some favor Solomon as author of the entire section while others hold that sages or unnamed wise men may have also contributed.

Interpreting Proverbs

Interpreting biblical poetry involves discovering how the author used parallel arrangements, Figures of Speech, images and other keywords.

1. Identify the type of parallelisms the author is using.

   - Determine use of Connecting Words (see appendix).

   - Ask, "How does the second line relate to the first line?" See parallelism list.

2. Develop Exegetical Outline based on parallelisms (see VISA 5).

3. Interpret the passage.

   - Ask and answer exegetical questions.

   - Consult reference tools: commentary, Bible dictionary, Bible encyclopedia, concordance, study Bible and word study tools (see appendix).

4. Revise the Exegetical Outline.

5. Paraphrase the passage.

6. Write the passage commentary (see appendix).

7. Develop Theological Outline (see Theological Interpretation in VISA 6).

Parallelism

Definition

Parallelism is the verse form of poetic literature that communicates meaning through the relationships of its lines.

Discussion

Parallelisms are patterned in pairs or triplets of lines to strategically, emotionally and powerfully express meaning.

Description

- Synonymous Parallelism: The second line expresses the same thought as the first line using different words (11:25; 19:5).

- Antithetical Parallelism: The second line contrasts the thought of the first line (10:2,3).

- Synthetic Parallelism: The second line expands the thought of the first line by adding a complementary thought. Sometimes it gives the reason (4:23; 16:3).

- Climatic Parallelism: The second line repeats part of the first line and extends the thought building up to a climatic statement (6:16-19; 30:15-16; Psalms 29:1-2).

- Emblematic Parallelism: A metaphor or simile in the first or second line explains the thought expressed in the other line (3:12b; Psalm 42:1; 103:13).

- Formal Parallelism: The second line simply completes the first line (21:16; Psalm 48:2).

Example

Exegetical Notes: Proverbs 3:5-6

⁵Trust in the LORD with all your **heart**

And do not **lean** on your own own understanding.

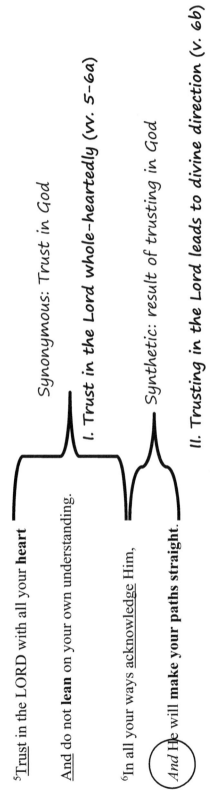

⁶In all your ways acknowledge Him,

And He will **make your paths straight.**

Synonymous: Trust in God

I. Trust in the Lord whole-heartedly (vv. 5-6a)

Synthetic: result of trusting in God

II. Trusting in the Lord leads to divine direction (v. 6b)

Key Words

- "trust" means to depend and rely on God
- "heart" refers to the seat of one's mind, will and emotions (figure of speech).
- "And" in verse 5 merely connects the first and the second lines together.
- "acknowledge" means to recognize the trustworthiness of God.
- "And" in verse 6 is a result connecting word expressing the principle that trusting God results in Him giving divine direction

Paraphrase: *Solomon told his son to rely on God and not to put any conference in himself. Obeying this command expressed in three different ways would result in God giving divine assistance.*

Exploration

Interpret the following passages.

1. Proverbs 11:22

2. Proverbs 3:31-32

3. Proverbs 7:1-5

4. Proverbs 12:16

5. Proverbs 30:24-28

Psalms

Definition

The Psalms are sacred collections of Hebrew poetry written by different authors over centuries intended to be sung with musical accompaniment in worship to God.

Discussion

The Psalms was Israel's hymn book. Its Hebrew title *Tehillim* means "book of praises." The English title comes from the Greek word *Psalmoi* (songs) found in the Septuagint.

The Psalms are arranged in five separate divisions: Book I. (1-41), Book II. (42-72), Book III. (73-89), Book IV. (90-106) and Book V. (107-150).

Generally speaking, the Psalms fall into certain types that share a distinct structure and format. Usually, the first line of the Psalm indicates its type. Although individual Psalms fall into particular types, they don't always fit rigidly into the format of those recognized types.

Lament Psalms: prayers to God from one experiencing persecution and trouble

Call	The psalmist calls out to God for help.
Cry Out	The psalmist laments about the situation of distress.
Confidence	The psalmist states confidence in God to intervene.
Petition	The psalmist gives a specific request for help.
Praise/Proclamation	The psalmist promises to respond to God's goodness.

Declarative Praise Psalms (Thanksgiving): thanks and appreciation given to God for deliverance from distress

Introduction	The psalmist states the intention to praise God or offers a praise to God.
Body Distress Cry for Help Deliverance	The psalmist reflects on a past need for God's help and reports on God's deliverance.
Conclusion	The psalmist restates his intention to praise God, offers praise to God or instructs others to praise God.

Descriptive Praise Psalms (Hymns): expression of specific reason for praising God and call for others to do so as well

Call to Praise	The psalmist commands others to praise God.
Cause for Praise	The psalmist gives reason (s) for praise to God.
Concluding Call to Praise	The psalmist reemphasizes his call to praise God.

Didactic Psalms: Communicate important lessons and teaching for God's people

Psalm Types

Types	Psalms
Lament	3, 4, 5, 6, 7, 9, 10, 11, 12, 13, 14, 15, 16, 17, 18, 23, 22, 25, 26, 27, 28, 31, 35, 36, 38, 39, 40, 41, 42,43, 51, 44, 45, 46, 53, 51, 54, 55, 56, 57, 58, 59, 60, 61, 62, 63, 64, 69, 70, 71, 74, 77, 79, 80, 82, 83, 85, 86, 88, 90, 94, 102, 106, 108, 109, 115, 120, 121, 123, 125, 129, 130, 131, 137, 139, 140, 143
Declarative Praise Psalms (Thanksgiving)	18, 21, 22, 30, 32, 34, 52, 65, 66, 67, 68, 75, 92, 107, 116, 118, 124, 126, 129, 138
Descriptive Praise Psalms (Hymns)	2, 8, 15, 18, 19, 20, 21, 24, 29, 33, 36, 42, 43, 44, 45, 46, 47, 48, 50, 66, 68 72, 74, 76, 77, 78, 80, 81, 83, 84, 87, 89, 91, 93, 95, 96, 97, 98, 99, 100, 101, 103, 104, 105, 106, 107, 110, 111, 113, 114, 117, 120, 121, 122, 123, 124, 125, 126, 127, 128, 129, 130, 131, 132, 133, 134, 135, 136, 144, 145, 146, 147, 148, 149, 150
Didactic	1, 9, 10, 15, 19, 25, 34, 36, 37, 49, 62, 73, 82, 91, 94, 111, 112, 119, 123, 127, 133, 134, 145

Interpreting Psalms

Interpreting Psalms requires the Bible student to pay special attention to historical context, type of Psalm, parallel arrangement, use of words, images and Figures of Speech.

Preparation

1. Review the historical context of the Psalm (when possible).

   - See commentaries & special studies on Psalms.

   - See *Psalm Helps* by Dr. Richard Klein.

Process

2. Determine the type & structure of the Psalm.

3. Develop an Exegetical Outline according to the type (when possible).

4. Identify parallelism used throughout the psalm.

5. Interpret the Psalm.

   - Ask and answer exegetical questions.

   - Consider various contexts: cultural, historical and literary.

   - Consult reference tools: commentary, Bible dictionary, Bible encyclopedia, concordance, study Bible and word study tools (see appendix).

6. Revise the Exegetical Outline.

7. Paraphrase the passage.

8. Write the passage commentary (see appendix).

9. Develop Theological Outline (see Theological Interpretation in VISA 6).

Example

Exegetical Notes: Psalm 100

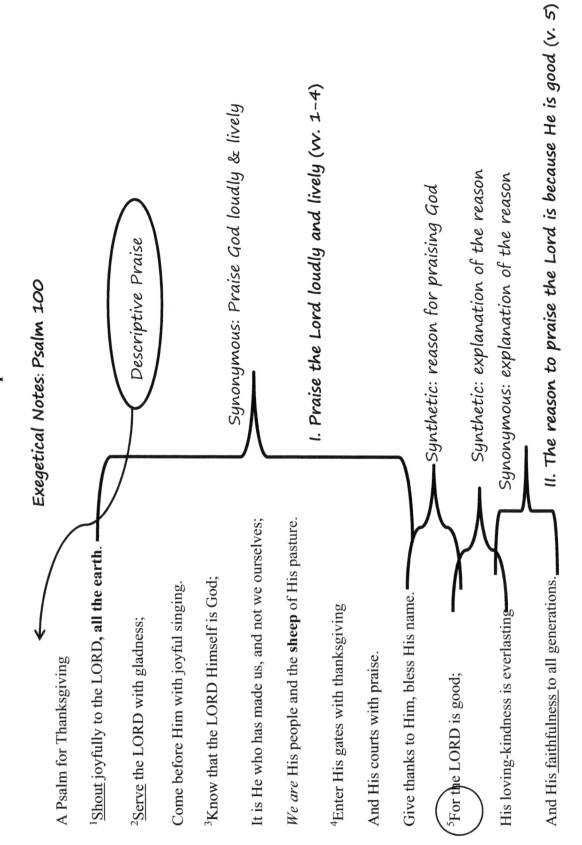

Descriptive Praise

A Psalm for Thanksgiving

¹Shout joyfully to the LORD, **all the earth.**

²Serve the LORD with gladness;

Come before Him with joyful singing.

³Know that the LORD Himself is God;

It is He who has made us, and not we ourselves;

We are His people and the **sheep** of His pasture.

⁴Enter His gates with thanksgiving

And His courts with praise.

Give thanks to Him, bless His name.

⁵For the LORD is good;

His loving-kindness is everlasting

And His faithfulness to all generations.

Synonymous: Praise God loudly & lively

I. Praise the Lord loudly and lively (vv. 1–4)

Synthetic: reason for praising God

Synthetic: explanation of the reason

Synonymous: explanation of the reason

II. The reason to praise the Lord is because He is good (v. 5)

Keywords

- "shout" (v.1) means to raise the voice and pearce the air with sound.

- "all the earth" (v.1) refers to Gentile nations (figure of speech)

- "serve" (v. 2) means to exude physical energy in service to God.

- "sheep" (v. 3) refers to the Israelites as a group of people who God takes care of (figure of speech)...

- "For" (v. 5) is a causal connecting word that gives the reason for praising God.

- "faithfulness" (v. 5) refers to God's trustworthiness and dependability.

Paraphrase

The Psalmist gives 8 synonymous comannds to praise and worship God. The reason he calls on all the earth to praise God is because as the creator and caretaker of all, He is good. His goodness is reflected in His merciful kindness and His enduring trustworthiness.

Exploration

Interpret the Psalms below.

1. Psalms 1

2. Psalms 3

3. Psalms 13

4. Psalm 30

5. Psalm 70

Itinerary

- Become familiar with the elements of narratives

- Learn the process of interpreting narratives

- Practice interpreting narrative passages

VISA 8: Interpreting Narratives

Narratives

Definition

Narratives refer to that form of literature which conveys events made up of setting, characters, plot, and narrator's point of view for the purpose of teaching biblical truth. Simply put narratives are stories told to communicate theological principles.

Discussion

Narratives make up the dominant form of biblical literature. This evidences the fact that God works in, on, with, for and through the lives of people. The function of a narrative is to communicate truth through meaningful accounts of God's interaction with people. Rather than telling us how to think, feel or act as do the Epistles, narratives show us the thinking, feeling and acting of others and by implication how we should model or avoid following suit. Instead of commanding us to trust God whole-heartedly, Genesis gives us the story of Abraham trusting as well as not trusting God. Narratives show us a picture of God, man and life in action.

Description

17 Old Testament and five New Testament books fit in the general category of narrative literature (see Literary Forms in the appendix). However, many other Old Testament books though characterized as other types of literature are in large part stories.

The essential features of narrative literature are:

- Setting

- Characters

- Plot

- Narrator

Setting

Definition

Setting refers to the temporal, historical, geographical, physical, cultural and theological circumstances and conditions of a story.

Discussion

The setting of a narrative acts similar to stage direction in a play and gives credibility and authenticity to the story. Setting makes it possible to understand the activities of the story.

Description

The setting of a story may be expressed in several different ways.

- Temporal: Refers to specific time aspects such as day, night and immediate moments in time (Gen. 32:22-24; Matt. 14:25; Luke 23:44).

- Historical: Refers to more significant time periods or larger timeline related to the events of the story (Josh. 4:19; Neh. 1:1; John 13:1).

- Geographical: Refers to locales related to the story's actions such as cities, regions, seas, mountains, etc. (1 Sam. 21:9; Matt. 3:5-6; Acts. 1:8).

- Physical: Refers to a specific material places such as synagogues, houses, boats, etc. (Gen. 37:24; 1 Sam. 22:1; Luke 19:4).

- Cultural: Refers to the social norms and values that influenced human interaction (Isa. 20:2; Mark 9:36-37; John 4:7-9).

- Theological: Refers to how people worshipped and related to God and how He related to them (Ex. 13:21; 2 Sam. 24:11-13; Mark 3:2-4).

Characters

Definition

Characters refer to the individuals who populate and produce the action of the story.

Discussion

Information for understanding characters in biblical narratives is set forth in the following ways:

- by the narrator's description (Num. 12:3; Matt. 1:19; Acts 11:24)

- by the Character's attitude and actions (Psalm 51:1-4; Amos 7:2,5; Luke 23:34)

- by other's attitudes and actions toward the character (Num. 11:11-13; Luke 23:42; Rev. 5:9-14)

Types & Roles

Characters are deliberately portrayed according to types and roles. Type refers to how much and what kind of information is given on a character while role refers to how the character functions within the narrative.

Types	Functions
Round Characters have many traits: positive and negative (Jacob, David, Peter, Saul)	Protagonist: main character portrayed in positive light (God, David, Paul)
Flat Characters have a consistent trait (Rachel, Laban, Elizabeth)	Antagonist: opposes the protagonist (Jonah, Saul, Pharisees)
Agents have no particular personality (multitude, servants)	Foil: characters used to contrast another character (Hagar, Laban, Pilate)

Plot

Definition

Plot refers to the meaningful unfolding of a story from beginning to middle to end.

Discussion

Plot refers to what the story is about. It is concerned with how the events of a story are arranged and organized to communicate meaning. It ties individual episodes into a coherent story. For example, in the Jacob narrative, we see numerous episodes (Rebekah's inquiry of God, Jacob and the birthright, Jacob's ladder, Laban tricks Jacob and God wrestling with Jacob). All of these separate and distinct events make up the larger story of God fulfilling his promise to Abraham through Jacob despite His human frailties.

The plot of a story is driven by conflict. Conflict is the tension between the present reality (usually negative) and the ideal state of the main character.

A narrative maybe arranged in one of two types of plot structure.

- In a Peak Plot, the conflict of a story crescendos to a single event where the tension is broken and declines to the end of the story.

- In a Plateau Plot, the conflict of a story progresses not to a single event but through a series of events and declines to an end.

Description

Peak Plot Structure
Gospel of Mark

Climax (15:33-47)

Result
(16:1-18)

Conflict Developed
(8:27-15:32)

Conclusion

(16:19-20)

Conflict Introduced
(2:8-26)

Introduction

(1:1-45)

66

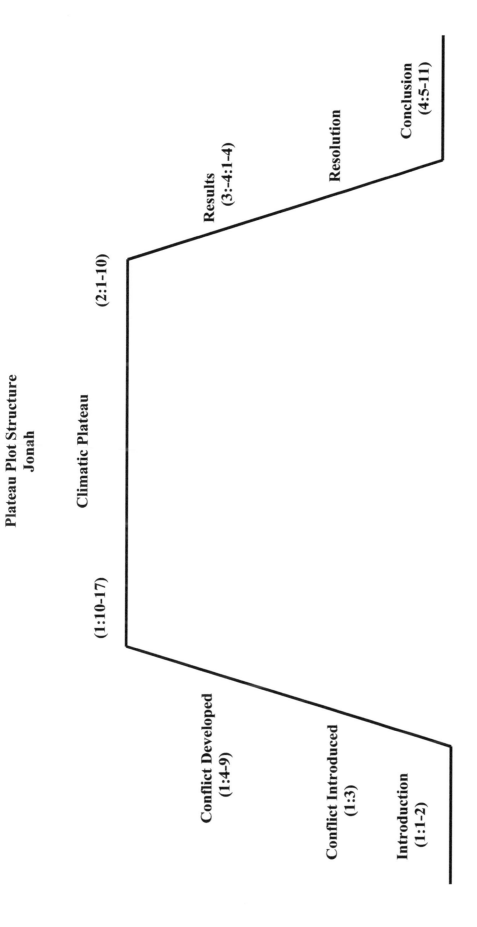

Plateau Plot Structure
Jonah

Climatic Plateau

(1:10-17)

(2:1-10)

Results
(3:-4:1-4)

Resolution

Conclusion
(4:5-11)

Conflict Developed
(1:4-9)

Conflict Introduced
(1:3)

Introduction
(1:1-2)

67

Narrator

Definition

The narrator refers to the individual giving the account of the narrative or the person telling the story.

Discussion

The narrator provides direction and perspective for understanding the meaning of the events of the story. The narrator's point of view gives the perspective from which the actions of the story should be understood (positive, negative, etc.)

Description

In order to express a story with meaning, a narrator takes on the following traits:

- Omniscient (knows all of the events of the story):

- Omnipresent (ever present at all the events of the story):

- Omni-temporal (aware of all the times related to the story):

Interpreting Narratives

Interpreting narratives involves discovering the meaning or significance of the author's use of the above elements as well as how he used particular words and phrases. This investigation is the means to the end. Ultimately, you are trying to answer the questions: What does this story teach me about God? What does this story teach me about man? What does this story teach me about life in general?

Preparation

1. Learn the story.

   - Read the story several times.

   - Write a brief synopsis of the story.

2. Develop an Exegetical Outline (see VISA 5). ✎

Process

3. Interpret the story.

   - Investigate the various settings of the story. Consult several commentaries, Bible dictionaries, Bible encyclopedias, Bible atlases and Bible handbooks.

   - Chart the characters of the story and make note of their attitudes and actions. Determine implications of their attitudes and actions: What do their thoughts, feelings, words and behavior teach you about them? What do the thoughts, feelings, words and behavior of others in relation to a particular character teach you about that character? How does the text describe characters? Remember, don't factor God out of the story.

   - Determine how the narrator portrays the action of the characters (point of view): positive, negative or neutral.

   - Ask and answer exegetical questions.

   - Identify and determine the meaning of keywords used in the passage. Keywords maybe spoken by a character or mentioned by the narrator.

4. Revise the Exegetical Outline.

5. Paraphrase the passage.

6. Write the passage commentary (see appendix).

7. Develop Theological Outline (see Theological Interpretation in VISA 6).

Description

Joshua 4:19-24
Settings

Historical	Israel crossed the Jordan 40 years to the day that God instructed them to prepare to leave Egypt (Exod. 12:3). He proved His faithfulness.
Geographical	Jordan River: mentioned in the O.T. as a boarder; the crossing of the Jordan gave Israel entry into the land of promise. Gilgal: a town near Jericho gave Israel its first foothold in the land of promise.
Cultural	In the Near East, stacking stones was often considered a covenant ritual.
Theological	The Ark of the Covenant, which symbolized God's presence went before the people to show that it was God providing the miracle of stopping the waters of the Jordan from flowing (3:11).

Characters

Character	Actions & Attitudes	Implications
Joshua	Set up 12 stones at Gilgal. Told Israel to use the stones as a memorial to God's greatness.	He was obedient to God. Expressed high reverence for God.
The People	Came up from the Jordan. Camped at Gilgal. Took stones from the Jordan.	They were obedient to God. They were obedient to Joshua.
The Lord	Dried the waters of the Jordan. Dried the waters of the Red Sea.	God provided for His people to do His will.

Plot: Obeying God, Joshua launched the campaign to conquer the land of promise. The first objective in the campaign was to cross the Jordan River Jordan (1:2; 3:1-5:1).

Point of View: Joshua, the people and the Lord's actions are portrayed positively.

Keywords

Keyword	Meaning/Use	Implications
that (v. 24)	purpose connecting word giving the goal or intent for God bringing Israel across the Red Sea and the Jordan River	God had a deliberate purpose and plan for blessing Israel.
peoples (v.24)	refers to pagan nations when used in the Old Testament	God blessed Israel for a greater purpose than social liberation but that all the unbelieving nations would recognize His power on behalf of His people. God is sovereign over the unbelieving nations.
so that (v. 24)	purpose connecting word giving the goal or intent for God bringing Israel across the Red Sea and the Jordan River	God had an additional purpose for blessing Israel.
fear (v. 24)	To reverence God and be faithful to Him	God's additional purpose was to draw Israel's perpetual devotion.

Paraphrase

Forty years to the day after God instructed Israel to prepare to leave Egypt, Joshua and the younger generation crossed the Jordan River and camped at Gilgal near Jericho. Joshua set up the twelve stones that God commanded him to have taken out of the Jordan. After setting up the stones, Joshua spoke to the people regarding the significance of his actions. Knowing the stones would be the object of inquisition by their children, Joshua instructed Israel to remind them of their God saturated culture. He told them to rehearse to their children how God provided deliverance for them from Egypt by the crossing of the Red Sea and how God provided for their promise by the crossing of the Jordan. They are to instruct their children that these provisions were not for the sake of Israel. Rather it was so that the entire world would know that the Lord is mighty and that Israel would stay true to Him forever.

Exploration

Interpret the following narrative passages.

1. Numbers 21:1-9

2. Judges 17:1-13

3. Haggai 2

4. Luke 6:6-11

5. Acts 14

...an earthly story with a heavenly meaning.

-Unknown-

Itinerary

- Learn how parables work

- Develop personal confidence in interpreting parables

- Practice interpreting parables

VISA 9: Interpreting Parables

Parables

Definition

Parables are figurative stories conveying spiritual truth.

Discussion

Parables have the distinction of being narrative in form but figurative in function. The term comes from the Greek word *paráballō* which means to compare or place side by side. Parables lift up comparisons in order to inform, inspire and instruct. Some have been called extended similes because they make clear and direct comparisons ("the Kingdom of Heaven is like…") while others have been called extended metaphors because their comparisons are not so clear or direct. Though figurative, parables are true-to-life yet non-historical stories where their historicity has no bearing on their meanings.

Jesus used parables to answer questions, address issues and solve problems. Their two fold purpose was to reveal truth to His followers and to conceal truth from those who rejected Him (Mark 4:11). Jesus' parables are found in the first three Gospels. Though scholars disagree on their exact number, Luke is credited with having the greatest number with at least 15 being unique to his writing. Matthew is second with at least 11 unique to his writing and Mark follows with at least two unique to his writing.

Although parables express a dominant truth, they do not conform to a single structural arrangement. Some are very brief, simple and straightforward while others are a bit long and quite complex. They do however evidence patterns of interaction between characters. Some parables have three main characters with a triangular pattern of interaction. A unifying character, usually in an authoritative role (father, king, master) interacts with two subordinate main characters or groups (sons, slaves, servants) who have contrasting attributes or responses to him.

Some parables have two main characters or groups where two different types of patterns can be traced: (1) a horizontal pattern where two people in the same or similar social class display contrasting attitudes or actions and (2) a vertical pattern where one in superior rank interacts with one or others of inferior rank.

Other parables tend to focus on a single element or object and tend to be direct or implied comparisons.

Use the list below to identify parables and their patterns.

Parable Patterns

Pattern	Parable	Passage
1. Direct Comparison	Mustard Seed	Matthew 13:31-32 Mark 4:30-32 Luke 13:18-19
2. Direct Comparison	Leaven	Matthew 13:33 Luke 13:20-21
3. Direct Comparison	Hidden Treasure	Matthew 13:44
4. Direct Comparison	Pearl of Great Price	Matthew 13:45-46
5. Direct Comparison	Fishing Net	Matthew 13:47-50
6. Direct Comparison	Growth of The Seed	Mark 4:26-29
7. Direct Comparison	Rude Children	Luke 7:31-35
8. Direct Comparison	Lost Sheep	Matthew 18:12-14 Luke 15:4-7
9. Direct Comparison	Lost Coin	Luke 15:8-10
10. Direct Comparison	Unworthy Slave	Luke 17:7-10
11. Horizontal	Wise & Foolish Builders	Matthew 7:24-27 Luke 6:47-49
12. Horizontal	Good Samaritan	Luke 10:25-37
13. Horizontal	Pharisee & Tax Collector	Luke 18:9-14
14. Indirect Comparison	New Cloth & New Wine Skins	Matthew 9:16-17 Mark 2:21-22 Luke 5:36-39
15. Indirect Comparison	Friend at Midnight	Luke 11:5-8
16. Indirect Comparison	Barren Fig Tree	Luke 13:6-9
17. Indirect Comparison	Great Banquet	Luke 14:15-24

18. Indirect Comparison	Tower Builder & Warring King	Luke 14:28-33
19. Indirect Comparison	Shrewd Manager	Luke 16:1-9
20. Triangle	Sower, Seed & Soil	Matthew 13:5-8 Mark 4:3-8 Luke 8:5-8
21. Triangle	Wheat & Tares	Matthew 13:24-30
22. Triangle	Vineyard Workers	Matthew 20:1-16
23. Triangle	Two Sons	Matthew 21:28-32
24. Triangle	Two Slaves	Matthew 24:45-51 Luke 12:42-48
25. Triangle	10 Virgins	Matthew 25:1-13
26. Triangle	Talents	Matthew 25:14-30
27. Triangle	Prodigal Son	Luke 15:11-32
28. Triangle	Minas	Luke 19:11-27
29. Vertical	Rich Fool	Luke 12:16-21
30. Vertical	Wicked Tenants	Matthew 21:33-46 Mark 12:1-12 Luke 20:9-19
31. Vertical	Unforgiving Slave	Matthew 18:23-35
32. Vertical	Wedding Banquet	Matthew 22:1-14
33. Vertical	Door Keeper	Mark 13:34-37
34. Vertical	Two Debtors	Luke 7:41-43
35. Vertical	Unjust Judge	Luke 18:1-8

Interpreting Parables

When interpreting the parables, keep in mind that you're studying a story within a story. The evangelists stepped back and allowed Jesus to momentarily become the story teller.

Preparation

1. Identify the type of parable you're studying.

2. Read the story several times.

3. Develop an Exegetical Outline.

Process

4. Identify the setting.

   - Occasion: What is the question, problem or situation that prompted the parable?

   - Historical Setting: Who is the parable spoken to? Why?

   - Cultural Setting: What social norms and factors influence the events of the story?

5. Understand the story's natural/literal meaning.

   - Ask and answer exegetical questions.

   - Identify and determine the meaning of keywords used in the passage. Keywords maybe spoken by a character or mentioned by the narrator.

   - Investigate any references/allusions related to the parable in other passages.

   - Consult reference tools: commentary, Bible dictionary, Bible encyclopedia, concordance, study Bible and word study tools (see appendix).

6. Revise the Exegetical Outline.

7. Paraphrase the passage.

8. Write the passage commentary (see appendix).

9. Develop Theological Outline (see Theological Interpretation in VISA 6).

Description

Matthew 25:14-30

Story

Setting	Occasion: the disciples' question about the sign of the Lord's 2nd Coming (Matt. 24:3) Historical: the disciples are addressed about how they are to respond in light of the Lord's departure and return Cultural: masters regularly traveled and left possessions to slaves, the money could have been invested and doubling it was normal and expected
Natural Meaning	A man goes on a journey, entrusts his slaves with his possessions at differing levels; two of the slaves traded and increased what was given to them and one did not; the master returned to settle accounts and rewarded two slaves while condemning the other

Paraphrase

Jesus answered the disciples' question about His return by giving a parable. A master went on a journey and entrusted his possessions to his slaves at varying levels. Two of the slaves pleased the master by doing what was expected with the talents. They served for his benefit. One servant did not. He did not advance the master's interest. The master rewarded the two slaves that did what he intended them to do and condemned the one who did not. The master expected the slaves to increase what he had given them for his benefit and responded to the slaves according to their faithfulness to his will. This is what the 2nd Coming is like; not knowing when the master will return but expected to advance His interest until He comes. When He comes He will settle accounts.

Exploration

Interpret the parables below.

1. Matthew 13:44

2. Matthew 13:24-30

3. Mark 13:33-37

4. Luke 13:6-9

5. Luke 18:1-8

You will find a no more fascinating and rewarding experience than to trace in the lines of real men and women the fusion of God's divine providence with the human personality.

-Alan B. Stringfellow-

Itinerary

- Understand the benefits of studying a Bible personality

- Learn the process of biographical study

- Glean personal life lessons from studying the life of a Bible character

VISA 10: Biographical Study

Biographical Study

Definition

Biographical Study refers to discovering biblical truth through investigating the life of a Bible personality.

Discussion

Indeed God teaches theological principles or life lessons from the lives of other people. It is beneficial then for the Bible student to develop an appreciation for and skill in studying the lives of Bible personalities. A Biographical Study explores a Bible character's **LIFE**.

- **L**egacy (role in biblical history, ministry, success, failure, death)
- **I**ndividuality (character assessment: good, bad, social status, conversion)
- **F**ellowships (nature of relationships with friends, family, etc.)
- **E**arly Life (birth through young adult years, hometown, etc.)

Process

1. Collect biblical information on the character.

   - Use ONLY a concordance and a Bible.
   - Note: The person may have more than one name or title.
   - Note: There may be more than one person with the same name.

2. Categorize biblical information on the character.

   - Take four blank sheets of paper and label each of them with one of the headings: Legacy, Individuality, Fellowships, and Early Life.

   - Read each Scripture reference on the character in its context (paragraph). Remember that Scripture gives information on Bible personalities in three ways:

     - by direct description (Num. 12:3; Matt. 1:19; Acts 11:24)
     - by the Character's attitude and actions (Gen. 25:29-33; Amos 7:2,5; Luke 23:34)
     - by other's attitudes and actions toward the character (Num. 11:11-13; Luke 23:42; Rev. 5:9-14)

   - Ask: "What does the passage teach me about this person?"

     - Write descriptive thoughts about the character on the appropriate worksheets. Don't be overly concerned about the exactness of where your descriptions should be placed. You can settle any doubt after you record all of the biblical data. Be sure to include Scripture references at the end of your statements/phrases.

- Note: Scripture may not contain information for one or more of the four categories on a particular character.

- After you have recorded all biblical data, review the worksheets and determine the appropriate category for thoughts you may have been confused about. Thoughts cannot be repeated in any category.

  - Cut duplicated or repeated comments.

  - Combine and summarize similar thoughts. Indicate all of the related Scripture references.

3. Catalog biblical information on the character.

   - Write a one page Biographical Outline from your worksheets (see example on next page).

   - Develop Major Points according to the following pattern:

     - I. Legacy
     - II. Individuality
     - III. Fellowships
     - IV. Early Life

     - Give each Major Point a title (2-5 words).

   - Develop Minor Points and Sub-Points of the Outline.

     - Minor Points which are specific representations of Major Points are indicated by alphabets (A., B., C., D., E., etc.). A Minor Point A requires a Minor Point B.

     - Sub-Points which refer to specific representations of Minor Points are indicated by Arabic numbers (1., 2., 3., 4., etc.). A Sub-Point 1 requires a Sub-Point 2.

   - Summarize the character's life in one complete sentence (20 words or less).

   - Title the outline.

Presentation

4. Communicate biblical information on the character.

   - Write a one page to two page commentary on the life of the character.

   - List at least three life lessons (theological principles) from you study.

Note: After you have completed your study, consult a Bible Dictionary, Bible Encyclopedia or character study to validate your discoveries.

Description

Jacob: Confessions of a Crooked Stick

Exegetical Big Idea: Jacob was an unfaithful man whom God opposed and later favored for is humility.

I.   The Tradition of Jacob
   A.   Fathered the fathers of the 12 tribes of Israel (Gen. 35:23)
   B.   Had a divine destiny prior to birth (Gen. 25:23)
   C.   Acknowledged his troubled life (Gen. 47:9)
   D.   Died in Egypt at 147 years old (Gen. 46:1-7; 47:28)
   E.   Buried in Hebron in the cave purchased by Abraham (Gen. 50:13)

II. The Times of Jacob: Good-Bad-Ugly
   A.   Jacob's Terror
      1.   Was unnecessarily covetous (Gen. 25:31)
      2.   Was subject to wrongful influence (Gen. 27:6-13; 30:4)
      3.   Was conniving and deceptive (Gen. 25:29-33; 27:19,35; 31:20)
      4.   Was a self-centered heartbreaker (Gen. 27:38)
      5.   Name meant "heel grabber" or "supplanter" (Gen. 27:36)
   B.   Jacob's Transparency
      1.   Spiritually sensitive (Gen. 28:16-17)
      2.   Worshipped God (Gen. 28:18-19)
      3.   Honored God (Gen. 28:19)
      4.   Professed his faith in God (Gen. 28: 20-22)
   C.   Jacob's Triumph
      1.   Tenacious and persistent (Gen. 32:25-26)
      2.   Humble (Gen. 32:27)
      3.   Worthy of a new name (Gen. 32:28)
      4.   Spiritually reflective (Gen. 32:30)
      5.   Expressed devotion to God (Gen. 35:2-3,7,14)

III. The Tragedy of Jacob
   A.   Discounted by his father (Gen. 27:1-4)
   B.   Exploited by his mother (Gen. 27:8-10)
   C.   Hated by his brother (Gen. 27:41)
   D.   Deceived by his uncle (Gen. 29:21-25)
   E.   Heartbroken by his sons (Gen. 25:26)

IV. The Tree of Jacob
   A.   Grandson of Abraham (Gen. 25:19)
   B.   Son of Isaac and Rebekah (Gen. 25:21)
   C.   Youngest of twin boys (Gen. 25:26)

Exploration

Develop a Biographical Study on the following characters.

1. Epaphras

2. Abigail

3. John The Baptist

4. Jezebel

5. Timothy

6. Martha

... the epistle was an appropriate channel for sharing personal testimony and delivering exhortations and commands, in addition to interpreting the grand truths of the gospel.

-Irving L. Jensen-

Itinerary

- Become familiar with the features of the Epistles

- Learn the process of interpreting the Epistles

- Practice interpreting the Epistles

VISA 11: Interpreting the Epistles

Epistles

Definition

The Epistles are occasional letters written by particular authors to particular audiences in response to particular situations.

Discussion

21 of the 27 books of the New Testament are Epistles. 13 were written by the Apostle Paul and the remaining eight were written by the Apostle Peter, James, the Apostle John, Jude and an anonymous author.

	Pauline Epistles	General Epistles
Travel:	Galatians, 1 & 2 Thessalonians 1 & 2 Corinthians, Romans	Hebrews (anonymous)
		James (James)
Prison:	Philemon, Colossians, Ephesians	1 & 2 Peter (Peter)
	Philippians	1, 2, & 3 John (John)
Pastoral:	1 Timothy, Titus, 2 Timothy	Jude (Jude)

Although there are variations among the Epistles they share the following basic structure:

__Introduction__	__Body__	__Conclusion__
• Author	• Purpose Statement	• Closing Comments
• Audience	• Theological Discussions	• Praise/Prayer
• Greeting	• Warnings/Rebukes	
• Thanksgiving	• Exhortations	
	• Applications	

Interpreting the Epistles

Remember that unlike the series of events in narratives and the sequence of feelings in lyric poetry, the flow of the Epistles is more topical and/or logical. Thus they require an interpretive approach that fits their unique features. Along with other Exegetical Questions, the Bible student may employ the following phases of interpreting words: definition, rationale and implication.

Preparation

1. Note: the Mechanical Layout (Visa 4) is especially suited for asking and answering exegetical questions in epistolary literature.

2. Create an interpretation worksheet that includes three columns. Indicate the passage being studied and label the columns: Scripture, Questions and Answers as shown below.

Interpretation Worksheet: Colossians 2:16-19

Scripture	Questions	Answers
v. 16	Definition: judge Rationale: Implications:	

3. In the Questions column list the three phases as shown above.

4. Select a keyword or phrase to investigate (see Magnificent 7 in the appendix). Write the keyword or phrase in the Questions column next to the word Definition. Indicate the verse where the word or phrase appears in the Scripture column.

Process

5. Definition Phase: determine how the author used a word or phrase.

   - Answer the question, "What does this term or phrase mean in context?"

   - Consult word study tools listed in appendix.

   - Determine the author's use of the word or phrase be reviewing the paragraphs surrounding the word or phrase.

   - Write the correct usage of the word in the Answers column of the worksheet.

6. Rationale Phase: determine the reason the author used the word or phrase.

- Answer the question, "Why did the author use this term or phrase this way, to these people at this time?"

- Remember the purpose and occasion of the book.

- Search the context of the passage.

- Answer the question in your own words. You may use the Function Words list found in this lesson a verb that indicates the reason the author used a particular word or phrase.

- Write down the verse reference(s) where you found the answer to the question.

- Sometimes there could be more than one answer.

7. Implication Phase: determine what is suggested or implied by the author's REASON(S) for using the word or phrase. Although not explicitly stated, implications are the natural conclusions and legitimate inferences drawn from sound investigation of the text.

- Consider these questions:

- "What does this communicate about the author?"

- "What does this communicate about the audience?

- "What does this communicate about circumstances and conditions related to the passage?"

8. Repeat Steps 2-6 for each word or phrase that you want to investigate.

9. Revise the Exegetical Outline.

10. Paraphrase the passage.

11. Write the passage commentary (see appendix).

12. Develop Theological Outline (see Theological Interpretation in VISA 6).

Cover Page

Colossians 2:16-19

Exegetical Big Idea: Paul told the Colossians to reject false teaching and false teachers as a result of their unique relationship with the supreme Christ.

Paraphrase

16. Therefore let no one hold undue authority over you when it comes to food, drink or particular times and days

17. things which lack inherent value but the real substance is found in Christ Himself.

18. Let no one continue to defraud you of your prize by leading you based on their own legalism, wayward thinking, selfish motives

19. and heretical practices with regards to Christ who is the Head of the church and the One who holds all things together.

Interpretation Worksheet: Colossians 2:16-19

Scripture	Questions	Answers
v. 16	Definition: judge	Verb. (*krinō*) to act as a judge. To pass unfavorable judgment on something or someone with the intention of influencing the attitudes and actions of people. To condemn with the desire to have authority in the lives of others. *(A Greek-English Lexicon of the New Testament and Other Early Christian Literature, Hebrew-Greek Key Word Study Bible)*
	Rationale:	Paul used this word to **WARN** the Colossians against allowing someone to hold undue authority in their lives since Christ was head over all rule and authority (Col. 2:10).
	Implications:	Paul wants the Colossians to remember that Christ is superior to all other authority and to avoid allowing anyone to supplant His rightful position.
v. 16	Definition: Therefore	Result Connecting Word. (*oun*); for that reason: in consequence *(New American Standard Exhaustive Concordance of the Bible Updated Edition, Merriam-Webster Dictionary and Thesaurus)*
	Rationale:	Paul used this word to **DIRECT** the Colossians to a proper response to human authority in light of their relationship with Christ (Col. 2:8-15).
	Implications:	The Colossians relationship to Christ should govern how they relate to everyone and everything else. Paul does not reject human authority, he is acting as an authority figure in his writing. He does highlight the fact that the Colossians are free to follow Christ and not be bound to false teaching.

v. 17	Definition: shadow	Noun. (*skia*). Metaphor. A representation of something real. A foreshadow: indication of a future event. A slight indication of something.
		The use of the metaphor shows the similarity between the lack of inherent value of food, drink, festivals new moons and Sabbath days and the lack of inherent value of a shadow.
		(New International Dictionary of New Testament Theology-Abridged, Analytical Lexicon to the Greek New Testament, Merriam-Webster Dictionary and Thesaurus)
	Rationale:	Paul used this word to **DESCRIBE** the lack of significance of "things" in verse 16 in comparison to Christ (Col. 2:16-17).
	Implications:	Paul wanted the Colossians to remember that the true focus of worship was Christ not the customs, rituals and traditions intended to point to Him. They were not to replace or rival Him.

Function Words

Definition

Function Words refer to verbs that indicate the reason an author used a particular word or phrase.

Discussion

Function Words describe the mindset of the author in his writing.

Description

The following list of verbs can be used to point out the reason an author or speaker used a particular word or phrase.

To admonish	To discourage	To protect
To apply	To encourage	To motivate
To challenge	To exhort	To rebuke
To charge	To explain	To show
To clarify	To express	To teach
To correct	To illustrate	To urge
To describe	To inform	To warn
To direct	To highlight	

Exploration

Interpret the following passages from the Epistles. Select focus words and phrases and answer interpretive questions for each. On a separate page, paraphrase the entire passage and summarize it in one complete sentence.

1. Hebrews 12:14-17

2. James 1:2-5

3. 1 Peter 3:1-8

4. Galatians 6:1-10

5. 1 Thessalonians 5:1-11

...words are like chess pieces on a chess board. Their importance and force are determined by their relationship to other pieces in the sentence and the paragraph.

-Darrell L. Bock-

Itinerary

- Become familiar with types of word studies

- Appreciate the importance of studying words in various contexts

- Practice developing word studies

VISA 12: Biblical Word Studies

Biblical Word Studies

Definition

A Biblical Word Study refers to tracing and interpreting the use of a word throughout all of Scripture or in isolated parts of Scripture.

Discussion

The purpose of a word study is to discover truth through investigating how biblical writers used particular words. There are two types of biblical word studies: Exhaustive and Selective.

- An Exhaustive Word Study investigates a word's use throughout the Old and New Testaments.

- A Selective Word Study investigates a word's use within the Old or New Testament, within a Bible book or as used by a particular writer.

Preparation

1. Become familiar with the tools needed for the word study: a Bible, Word Study Worksheet (found in this lesson) and word study reference books (see appendix). Consult at least two of the word study references works during your study.

Process

2. For an Exhaustive Study, choose a word for study. For help in deciding a target word, see the Magnificent 7 in the appendix or write a Mechanical Layout (VISA 4).

3. At the top of the Biblical Word Study Worksheet, record the type of study, the target word and the range of biblical material covered by your study (Old Testament, New Testament, Romans, the Apostle John's use of the word "light" etc.).

4. Locate your target word in a concordance that corresponds to the version of your Bible. Write the Scripture references, the target word and its Strong's Reference Numbers in the appropriate boxes on the worksheet. The Strong's numbers refer to the Hebrew and Greek words that correspond to your target word.

5. Use the Strong's numbers to locate your target word uses in the Old Testament (Hebrew) Lexicon found at the back of the concordance. Read the first Old Testament passage of the target word. Consult other word study tools to help determine how the word is being used in context. Record your answer in the "Meaning/Use" section of the worksheet. Interpret the use of the word. Don't simply restate it. Indicate how the writer or the speaker employed the target word.

In the "Paraphrase" section, rewrite the verse in your own words. Repeat this step for each Old Testament use of the target word. At the bottom of the worksheet make notes of recurring, dominant or significant themes, thoughts or subjects.

6. Using the New Testament word study tools, repeat Steps 4-5 for all of the non-Pauline books of the New Testament.

7. Repeat Steps 4-6 for all of the Paul's writings.

Presentation

8. Write the Old Testament section of the word study paper.

   - List your observations of how the word was used in each of the verses where it appeared.
   - Indicate it the verses.
   - Indicate the Strong's Reference Numbers.
   - Summarize the Old Testaments uses of the target word in 1-3 sentences.

9. Repeat Step 8 for writing the New Testament: non-Pauline literature section of word study paper.

10. Repeat Step 8 for writing the New Testament: Pauline literature section of the word study paper.

11. Based on your study of this word, list three life lessons/theological principles. In other words what did your study of this term teach you about God, man and/or life. Support your thoughts by validating them with other parts of Scripture (See Theological Outline in VISA 6).

12. For a Selective Study, simply isolate Steps 1-1 in a particular section of Scripture or on a particular author's use of a word.

Description

Biblical Word Study Worksheet

Type of Study: Exhaustive   **Word:** Transformed   **Scripture:** Romans 12:2   **Period:** Old & New Testaments

Scripture	Word/Ref. #	Mean/Use	Paraphrase
Ezk. 7:20	Transformed #7760	Change in function; temple ornaments were taken (by Judah) and used to make idols which were later worshipped	"And they **changed** [the intended use of the temple treasure] the beauty of His ornaments into pride, and they made the images of their abominations and their detestable things with it; therefore I will make it an abhorrent thing to them."
2 Cor. 3:18	Transformed #3339	God progressively changing the outward appearance of a believer into the image of Christ	"But we all, with unveiled face beholding as in a mirror the glory of the Lord, are being **changed** (progressively) into the same image from glory to glory, just as from the Lord, the Spirit."
Phil. 3:21	Transform #3345	Christ changing the appearance of the earthly body into a heavenly body	"who will **change** the (earthly) body of our humble state into conformity with the (heavenly) body of His glory, by the exertion of the power that He has even to subject all things to Himself."
Rom 12:2	Transformed #3339	Change of outward attitudes and actions based on an inner work	"And do not be conformed to this world, but be **changed** (from the inside) by the renewing of your mind, that you may prove what the will of God is, that which is good and acceptable and perfect."

Notes: The prevailing thought in the use of this word is "change"—in function, in appearance and in action. When brought on by man, it was bad but when brought on by God it was good.

Biblical Word Study Worksheet

Type of Study: _____   **Word:** _____   **Scripture:** _____   **Range:** _____

Scripture	Word//Ref.#	Meaning/Use	Paraphrase

Notes:

Exhaustive Biblical Word Study

"Transformed"
(#3339 *metamorphoō*)

Romans 12:2

^{2} And do not be conformed to this world, but be **transformed** by the renewing of your mind, that you may prove what the will of God is, that which is good and acceptable and perfect.

Old Testament Uses

- Change in intended use (Ezk. 7:20) (#7760 *sum* or *sim*)

Summary: The word was used once to express a difference in the intended use of the temple ornaments.

New Testament Uses

Paul's Writing

- Progressive change in the outward appearance/action of the believer into the image of Christ (2 Cor. 3:18) (#3339 *metamorphoō*)

- Christ's changing the earthly body of the believer into a heavenly body (Phil. 3:21) (#3345 *metashematizō*)

- Change in the believer's outward appearance/actions based on the inner working of God (Rom. 12:2) (#3339 *metamorphoō*)

Summary: The word is used in the New Testament three times to communicate a difference in the appearance or actions of the believer brought about by God.

Life Lessons

1. God brings about life transformation. (Rom. 12:2; John 10:10; Eph. 2:8-10)

2. Transformation is not automatic. (1 Cor. 3:1-9; Heb. 5:12; James 1:21-22)

3. The believer has a responsibility to participate in life transformation. (Rom. 12:2; James 1:21-27; 1 Pet. 1:16)

Exploration

Develop Word Studies on the following words.

1. Exhaustive: How is the word "ability" used throughout Scripture?

2. Exhaustive: How is the word "stricter" used throughout Scripture?

3. Selective: How does the Apostle Paul use "ashamed" in Romans and 2 Timothy?

4. Selective: How does the Apostle John's use "darkness" in the Gospel of John and 1 John?

5. Selective: How does the writer of Hebrews use "perfect?"

You can't really get to know the Word of God unless you apply it to your life... You can be a walking Bible encyclopedia with your head crammed full of biblical knowledge, but it won't do you any good if you don't apply it practically in daily living.

-Rick Warren-

Itinerary

- Be convinced of the need to apply Scripture

- Learn the process of applying Scripture

- Apply Scripture to specific personal situations

VISA 13: Application

Application

Definition

Application refers to the believer putting the truths of Scripture into practice in the specific circumstances and situations of their daily life. Simply put, application is active obedience to the Word of God.

Discussion

Knowledge and understanding are never the goals of studying Scripture (1 Cor. 8:1). The goal of our study is life change (1 Tim. 1:5). The acquisition of biblical information without the impact of life transformation is a holy abomination (Prov. 28:9). All that you have done to this point is useless if you don't follow through with obedience (1 Sam. 15:22). History is replete with men and women who have mastered the facts of the text but not the life of the text.

Process

Use the following steps to apply Scripture to the specific circumstances of your life.

1. Scrutinize: Use the Life Sheet (found near the end of this lesson) to record (be specific) the current circumstances/situations of your life. To scrutinize simply means to write down what's happening in your life. This is very personal. Nobody has to see this. So BE VERY HONEST with yourself and God.

   In the following example, specific circumstances are reflected in the physical/personal as well as the spiritual/friends and family areas of a person's life.

	Personal	Family & Friends
Physical	Dr. says that I have high blood pressure.	
Spiritual		Many of my friends are unsaved but I'm scared to share my faith with them.

2. Summarize (Exegetical Big Idea): Summarize your passage in a single complete sentence (20 words or less).

   - Remember to make reference to the author and audience. Ex. *"Paul told the Colossians…"*

   - Ask "What is the life lesson for the original audience?"

3. Principle-ize (Theological Big Idea): Restate the above summary as a general and universal principle. A principle is a statement of an abiding and enduring truth. Drop all historical and cultural references. Begin your statement with *"All Christians Should…"*

    -   Example:

        -   Exegetical: "**Moses told the Israelites** that God would bless their obedience."

        -   Theological: "**All Christians should know** that God blesses obedience."

4. Personalize: Apply the principle to a specific situation in your life as identified in Step 1 from the Life Sheet.

    -   Be prayerful about the specific situation to select as well about how God will want you to address it.

    -   Select one of the specific situations listed on your Life Sheet.

    -   Ask "Based on this principle, what will I do differently **(NOW!)** to deal with this specific situation to the greater glory of God?"

    -   Write down your answer (be very specific, be active, be honest, be open…be ready). Include in your application statement what you will do, how you will do it, when and where.

    -   Don't give a testimony, this is not about what you have already done or are currently doing but what you will do differently based on the principle of the text and the guidance of the Holy Spirit.

    -   Start your application by stating and briefly describing the circumstance or situation you are addressing. Be specific.

    -   Then give the specific action you will take to deal with the specific situation you described. Begin you statement with *"Therefore, I will…"*

Description

Philippians 1:9-11

Summarize (Exegetical Big Idea): Paul told the Philippians that he was praying for their spiritual maturity.

Principle-ize (Theological Big Idea): All believers should be spiritually mature. (Phil. 4:8-9; Col. 1:28; Eph. 4:11-16)

Personalize: Ken and I engaged in a heated argument regarding the type and volume of music as well as the temperature in the car when we drove a cross country two weeks ago. We have not spoken to each other since. Therefore I will demonstrate spiritual maturity by apologizing to Ken (**who**) for our disagreement (**situation**) and will seek restoration with him. I will apologize to him (**what**) Friday during dinner at his house (**when, where**). I will acknowledge that I offended him and express sincere regret for it (**How**). I will ask him to share with me those things I do that cause a gap between us. I will listen and not respond (for at least 24 hours) and will ask him to pray with me in considering what he shares.

James 1:19-27

Summarize (Exegetical Big Idea): James told the Jew believers to respond to their trials by embracing and obeying the Word of God.

Principle-ize (Theological Big Idea): All believers should respond to their trials by embracing and obeying the Word of God. (Jos. 1:1-9; Matt. 4:1-11; James 1:5)

Personalize: I abuse alcohol and have been doing it for years. Right now my life is unmanageable. Therefore, I will change my current course of disobedience of doing nothing about my drinking problem (**situation**). I will accept my pastor's help and let him connect me with a local recovery group (**what, how**). I will call him tomorrow at 8:00 am (**when**) and tell him that I want to start right-a-way.

Proverbs 3:5-6

Summarize (Exegetical Big Idea): Solomon told his son that complete dependence on God results in divine assistance.

Principle-ize (Theological Big Idea): All believers should know that complete dependence on God results in divine assistance. (Prov. 16:3; Phil. 4:6-7; Matt. 6:25)

Personalize: I have been offered a promotion with my company which will require me to move to New York. Therefore as it relates to whether or not I should accept the job offer (**situation**), I will depend on God (**what**) by asking Belinda, Angie and Kim to fast and pray with me (**who, how**) for the next 2 weeks (**when**). I will meditate 30 minutes each morning on Proverbs 3:5-6 (**what, when, how**) until I have clarity of God's will on this matter.

Life Sheet

	Personal	Family/Friends	Work	Other
Physical				
Spiritual				
Emotional				
Financial				
Mental				

Exploration

Apply your study from the following to specific circumstances and situations in your daily life.

1. Proverbs 16:3

2. Luke 13:6-9

3. Martha

4. Acts 14

5. 1 Corinthians 9:19-24

- Historical & Cultural Background Tools

- Word Study Tools

- Biblical Reference Tools

- Magnificent 7

- Connecting Words

- Figures of Speech

- Laws of Structure

- Literary Forms

- Commentary (Colossians 2:16-19)

Appendix

Historical & Cultural Background Reference Tools

Historical Background	Cultural Background
1. Bible Knowledge Commentary	1. IVP Bible Background Commentary
2. Expositor's Bible Commentary	2. Holman Bible Dictionary
3. Zondervan NIV Bible Commentary	3. New Bible Dictionary
4. IVP Bible Background Commentary	4. New International Bible Dictionary
5. Talk Thru The Bible	5. International Standard Bible Encyclopedia
6. Holman Bible Dictionary	6. Pictorial Encyclopedia of the Bible
7. New Bible Dictionary	7. Zondervan Illustrated Bible Background Commentary
8. New International Bible Dictionary	
9. International Standard Bible Encyclopedia	
10. soniclight.com (study notes)	

Word Study Reference Tools

Old Testament	New Testament
1. Exhaustive Concordance/Lexicon	1. Exhaustive Concordance/Lexicon
2. Hebrew-Greek Key Study Bible	2. Hebrew-Greek Key Study Bible
3. Theological Wordbook of the Old Testament	3. Practical Word Studies in the New Testament
4. New International Dictionary of Old Testament Theology & Exegesis	4. Theological Dictionary of The New Testament Abridged
5. The Brown-Driver-Briggs Hebrew & English Lexicon (use with Index to Brown, Driver & Briggs Hebrew Lexicon)	5. Analytical Lexicon of the New Testament (revised and update version)
6. IVP Dictionary of Biblical Imagery	6. The Analytical Lexicon to the Greek New Testament
7. English Dictionary	7. New International Dictionary of New Testament Theology Abridged Edition
	8. Complete Word Study Dictionary-New Testament
	9. A Greek-English Lexicon of the New Testament and Other Early Christian Literature (use with An Index to the Revised Bauer-Arndt-Gingrich Greek Lexicon 2nd Edition)
	10. IVP Dictionary of Biblical Imagery
	11. English Dictionary

Biblical Reference Tools

Commentaries	Bible Dictionaries
1. Bible Knowledge Commentary	1. New Bible Dictionary
2. Expositor's Bible Commentary	2. New International Bible Dictionary
3. IVP Bible Background Commentary	3. Holman Bible Dictionary
4. Zondervan NIV Bible Commentary	4. Easton's Bible Dictionary
5. New American Commentary	5. Harper's Bible Dictionary

Bible Encyclopedias	Bible Atlases
1. International Standard Bible Encyclopedia	1. Bible Atlas & Companion
2. Pictorial Encyclopedia of the Bible	2. The Moody Atlas of Bible Lands
3. Baker Encyclopedia of the Bible	3. Zondervan NIV Atlas of the Bible

Internet Resources	Manners & Customs
1. soniclight.com (study notes)	1. Illustrated Manners & Customs of the Bible
2. biblehub.com	2. Manners & Customs of the Bible
3. bibletools.com	3. New Manners & Customs of Bible Times

The Magnificent 7

Definition

The Magnificent 7 refers to keywords used in Scripture that warrant special attention for study.

Discussion

The Magnificent 7 are used throughout Scripture by all biblical writers and consist of seven types of word uses.

1. Connecting Words indicate relationships between words and thoughts (see the appendix).

2. Verbs indicate the action or state of being within a passage.

3. Nouns are significant people, places and things within a passage.

4. Figures of Speech are words that communicate something other than their natural meaning (see the appendix).

5. Religious Terms are words that express religious significance.

6. Rare/Unusual Terms are words that are not commonly used in Scripture.

7. Repeated Terms are words that are restated.

Description

The following are examples of how the Magnificent 7 are used in Scripture.

1. Connecting Words: *"For"* (Psalm 100)

2. Verbs: *"conformed"* (Rom. 12:2)

3. Subjects: "dogs" (Phil. 3:1)

4. Figures of Speech: *"shepherd"* (Psalm 23:1)

5. Religious Terms: *"Sabbath"* (Mark 3:2)

6. Rare/Unusual Terms: *"transformed"* (Rom. 12:2)

7. Repeated Terms: *"faith"* (Heb. 11)

Connecting Words

Definition

Connecting Words **TELL** (**T**-Temporal, **E**-Emphatic, **L**-Local, **L**-Logical) about the relationships between words, phrases, clauses and sentences.

Discussion

Some of the most powerful words in all of Scripture are the simple yet profound ones referred to as "connectives." Connecting Words help us understand how an author's thoughts relate to each other and allow us to see where the author places emphasis.

Description

There are four types of Connecting Words.

1. Temporal: words that express time (when, after, as, before, now, then, until, while): "after" (Mark 8:31)

2. Emphatic: words that express emphasis (indeed, behold, only, verily, truly, now): "behold" (1Sam. 30:3)

3. Local: words that relate to location (where, at, in, on, upon): "upon" (Acts 1:8)

4. Logical: words that express the direction or emphasis of the author's thinking:

   - Purpose: words that express intent or goal (that, so that, in order that): "that" (Col. 1:28)
   - Result: words that express outcome or consequence (so, then, therefore, thus, that, and, now): "and" (Prov. 3:5-6)
   - Reason/Cause: words that express grounds or basis (because, since, for): "For" (Psalm 100:5)
   - Comparison: words that express similarities (also, as, as—so, so as, just as, likewise): "as… so" (Psalm 42:1)
   - Contrast: words that express opposite thought (but, nevertheless, otherwise, yet, although, more than, either or, neither nor): "but" (Rom. 2:8)
   - Condition: words that point to a result based on certain circumstances (if, accept, unless, since): "if" (2 John 10)
   - Connective: words that add additional thoughts (and, straightway): "And" (Mark 5:43)
   - Series of Fact: words that introduce multiple people, places or things (both, first of all, finally, and, or, nor): "both" (1Cor. 4:5)
   - Content: a word expresses the content of a thought or speech (that): "that" (Phil. 1:9)
   - Explanatory: words that point to clarification of a previous thought (for, namely): "For" (Eph. 2:10)

Figures of Speech[3]

Definition

Expressions where words and phrases are used in nonliteral ways for rhetorical effect.

Discussion

Figures of Speech are used commonly throughout all of Scripture. The phrase comes from the Greek word *paroimia* (by word, common saying or proverb). Figures of Speech make:

- abstract thoughts concrete (a picture is worth a thousand words)

- communication memorable (an apple a day keeps the doctor away)

- communication impactful (roses are red, violets are blue…)

When trying to determine if a Figure of Speech is being employed, consider the following guidelines:

- Does the Bible say to consider the word or phrase figuratively? (Mark 4:14-20; 4:4-8)

- Does using the literal sense of the word or phrase make sense? (2 Cor. 3:15)

- Does using the literal sense of the word or phrase promote sin or contradiction of a clear passage of Scripture? (Luke 14:26; Mark 12:31)

---

[3] See *Figures of Speech Used in the Bible* by E.W. Bullinger for extensive treatment of figures throughout all of Scripture.

Description

Figures & Facts	Functions	Forms
Simile: an explicit comparison usually employing the words "as" or "like"	Comparison	Job 41:24; Ps. 42:1; 90:4; Matt. 23:27; Rev. 1:14
Metaphor: an implicit comparison where one thing is, acts like or represents the other (verbs will usually be in the "to be" form)	Comparison	Matt. 5:13; John 6:35; 8:12; 10:9,11; 14:6; 15:5
Metonymy: a substitution of a related noun or name by another noun or name (the substituted noun or name gets its meaning from the context)	Substitution	Gen. 42:38; Neh. 5:9; Ps. 7:9; 2 Cor. 3:15; Gal. 2:12
Synecdoche: a part of something is used to represent the whole or vice versa or the specific of something is used to represent the general or vice versa	Substitution	Ps. 118:10; 42:1; Matt. 16:17; Rom. 16:4
Personification: attributing human characteristics to non-human things	Substitution	Ps. 100:1; Prov. 1:20-21; Luke 19:38; Rom. 6:9; James 1:15
Anthropomorphism: attributing human characteristics or actions to God	Substitution	Gen. 6:6; Ps. 8:3; 31:2; 139:16; Jer. 3:8
Apostrophe: direct speech to an object as if it could answer or to someone absent as if they were there	Intensity	Deut. 32:1; Ps. 68:16; 1 Ki. 13:2; 1 Cor. 15:55
Rhetorical Question: a question that does not require a verbal response	Omission	Gen. 18:14; Rom. 6:1; 8:31
Hyperbole: deliberate exaggeration to emphasize a point	Overstatement	Deut. 1:28; Ps. 51:17; Mk. 10:25; Lk. 14:26; John 21:25
Oxymoron: combining opposite or contradicting terms	Inconsistency	Is. 58:10; Rom. 12:1; 2 Cor. 12:10; Phil. 3:19
Paradox: appearing to be opposite of what is normally understood or expressions that appear to contradict each other	Inconsistency	Mark 8:35; Lk. 18:14; 1 Cor. 1:25; 7:22

Laws of Structure

Definition

Laws of Structure are literary devices biblical writers used to arrange words and express thoughts.

Discussion

Laws of Structure express the relationships between words, phrases, clauses, paragraphs and sections.

Description

Functions	Features	Forms
Repetition	The reiteration of the same words, phrases, names, clauses, ideas, etc.	Heb. 11; Lev. 18:2, 4-6,12,30
Comparison	Showing the similarities of things or persons	Ps. 42:1; Rom. 4:1-8; 6:5; Heb. 5:1-10
Contrast	Showing the dissimilarities of things or persons	Ps. 1; Prov. 21:2, 5, 15; James 1:23-27
Interchange	The exchanging or alternation of certain elements	Mark 12:13-34;
Particularization	The movement from the general to the particular	Hab. 3; Mt. 6:1-18
Cause and Effect	The progression from cause to effect or from effect to cause	Ps. 100; Lk. 19:9-10
Introduction	The inclusion of the background or setting for events or ideas	Gen. 2:4-25; Lk. 15:1, 2
Rhetorical Questions	The author or speaker asks questions to which the answer should be obvious, sometimes followed by their answer	Rom. 6 & 7
Summarization	The use of a summary either preceding or following a unit of material	Jos. 12; Gen. 1:1; 2:4; Mt. 1:17;
Pivot or Turning Point	The subject matter is arranged so that it turns around or upon some one factor	Mark 8:29; Lk. 9:51
Climax	The arrangement of material in such a way as to progress to the highest point where conflicts are resolved and various strands are brought together	Job 38:1; Mark 15:33-41

Literary Forms

Forms	Facts	Old Testament		New Testament	
Narrative	Stories	**Moses** Genesis · Exodus Leviticus Numbers Deuteronomy	**History** Joshua · Judges Ruth 1,2 Samuel 1,2 Kings 1,2 Chronicles Ezra · Nehemiah Esther	**Gospels** Matthew · Mark Luke · John	Acts
Poetry	Imaginative writings using parallels, stanzas & Figures of Speech	Job · Psalms · Proverbs · Ecclesiastes Song of Solomon			
Prophetic	Proclamation of God through His prophet to His people about His promises & plans	**Major** Isaiah · Jeremiah Lamentations Ezekiel · Daniel	**Minor** Hosea · Joel Amos ·Obadiah Jonah · Micah Nahum Habakkuk Zephaniah Haggai Zechariah Malachi		
Epistle	Occasional letters written by particular people to particular people at particular times for particular reasons			**Paul** Romans 1,2 Corinthians Galatians Ephesians Philippians Colossians 1,2 Thessalonians 1,2 Timothy · Titus Philemon	**General** Hebrews James 1,2 Peter 1,2,3 John Jude
Apocalyptic	Revelation of God to His people through His prophet about His promises & plans	(Daniel 2; 7; 8; 10—12) (Ezekiel 37:1-14; 40:1—48:35) (Zechariah 1:7—6:8)		Revelation	

116

Commentary

Doctrinal Deviants
Colossians 2:16-20

Exegetical Big Idea: Paul told the Colossians to reject false teaching and false teachers as a result of their unique relationship with the supreme Christ.

Context

In the previous paragraph, Paul highlighted the supremacy of Christ. He explored several aspects: His person, His position, His power and His provision. He also indicated the unique relationship the Colossians enjoyed with Christ. They were subject to Him, complete in Him, saved by and united with Him. In verses 16-19, Paul shared how they should respond to false teachers as a result of their relationship to Christ. The false teachers were marked by three vices in particular. Two were discussed by Paul in this passage. The false teachers had a misguided focus (vv. 16-17), a misdirected devotion (vv. 18-19) and misinformed actions (20-23).

Misguided Focus

Paul told the Colossians they were not obligated to follow the misguided ways of the false teachers. In verse 16, he admonished them to let no one "judge" them. Here, "judge" (*krinō*) means to seek influence or authority in someone's life by criticizing or condemning them. The false teachers were pressuring the Colossians to submit to their strongly held positions related to Jewish customs and traditions. In their minds, Christ was insufficient for salvation. The Colossians would also need to observe Judaist rituals.

In verse 17, Paul characterized food, drink, festivals, new moons and Sabbath days (v.16) as a mere "shadow" (*skia*). A "shadow" here refers to that which points to something else. In relation to Christ, these cultural and religious aspects of life signified or indicated the fulfillment of what was to come in the person of Christ. Paul used this metaphor to show the lack of inherent significance in these "things" in comparison to Christ. He wanted the Colossians to remember that the true focus of worship was Christ not the religious elements that merely pointed to Him. They should not supplant or rival Him.

Misdirected Devotion

Paul admonished the Colossians to reject a second aspect of the false teachers and their teaching, namely their reverence for angels. In verse 18, he warned them to let no one "keep defrauding" them of their prize. "Defraud" (*katabrabeuō*) literally means to rob of a prize or condemn. It carries the image of a sports official who rules against an athlete thus depriving him of victory and prize. In view is the false teachers' blatant rejection of the position, power and provision of Christ. They took pleasure in the harsh treatment of the body as a legalistic way to gain merit with God. They promoted the worship of angels as divine mediators. They created their own way of spiritual transcendence through visions and rejected the headship of Christ (v. 19). For the Colossians to do anything short of rejecting the false teachers would put them in jeopardy of being disqualified and excluded from the prize.

OXYGEN Press

a resource. for life.

Ingram Content Group UK Ltd.
Milton Keynes UK
UKHW031303290623
424274UK00021B/446

9 780986 384103